The CLV Revolution

VALENTIN RADU

The CLV Revolution

Transform your eCommerce with Customer Value Optimization

VIDIA Publishing House
Bucharest, 2023

The CLV Revolution: Transform your eCommerce with Customer Value Optimization/Valentin Radu

Editorial team
Editor: Iulia Ichim
Illustrator: Ioana Olga Bejan

Descrierea CIP a Bibliotecii Naţionale a României
RADU, VALENTIN ECONOMIE
The CLV Revolution: Transform your eCommerce with customer value optimization/Valentin Radu. - Bucureşti: Editura Vidia, 2023
ISBN 978-606-8414-75-1

339.138

The CLV Revolution:
Transform your eCommerce with Customer Value Optimization
ISBN 978-606-8414-75-1

Address: OP 6 – CP 41 Bucharest
Internet: www.vidia.ro
e-mail: office@vidia.ro

Table of Contents

This is for all the underdogs that
think they'll never be good enough.

You're wrong.

You're move valuable than you think.

You're still being cooked.

Introduction

What I remember most from my two hours as a butcher is the smell, still very ripe in my mind many years later. I was barely sixteen years old. I had no desire to be a butcher. My mother had dragged me from the soccer field, taken me to the butcher shop, and told me it was time to make something of my life. In her eyes, I was wasting time on the soccer field and had no chance of becoming a professional footballer. Her thinking was right, even if her method was not. In Romania in the mid-1990s, money was scarce for many families, including ours. As far as my mother was concerned, my job was to get a job.

Once she left, the two men who ran the shop sized me up. They were both much bigger than me, their smocks covered in blood. I was small and not very strong in their eyes. After a moment of critique, one of them said, "Okay, kid, we'll help you make something of yourself." Then they laughed, led me to a far dank corner, and put me to work making meatballs: scooping, rolling, patting, rolling again, scooping, repeating, repeating, repeating until my arms were red up to the elbows. I had to breathe through my mouth because every breath through my nostrils made me want to gag. There was a clock on the wall, and I kept looking at it, which only made things go slower. An hour passed, and just as the second hour was almost through, the two butchers walked outside to smoke. I tossed my smock on the floor and ran as fast as I could back to the football field, still covered in blood.

Very rarely do our lives move in straight lines, especially our professional lives. Mine has been a zig-zag with plenty of false starts, abrupt stops, and wild turns. After seventeen jobs and building four very distinct companies, what I have found is that the number one job to do, above all else, is to create value for others.

With that in mind, *The CLV Revolution* is not about making meatballs or producing a product or service. It's about helping you create value for your customers: aligning what you sell and how you sell with what they need across their lifetime.

Two Ways to Grow a Company

To grow your company, you can focus the bulk of your energy on 1) trying to acquire new customers (acquisition) or 2) nurturing existing customers across their customer journey and applying what you learn about acquiring better customers toward creating and improving the messaging behind better products (lifecycle).

Perhaps you know this by now, but I want to be very clear: Acquisition marketing alone does not work long-term for all business models. If what you sell gets bought multiple times, it may work for short bursts, but in the long run, it's called "churn and burn" for a reason—you will burn yourself out.

Right now, you might be struggling to reach your company's goals. Perhaps the process of acquisition marketing that you've been relying on is no longer working. The market has changed. The COVID-19 pandemic has forced traditional retailers to grow the e-commerce side of their businesses and will continue to impact the way we will all do business for years to come. There is more competition than ever, and the internet and social media are changing as well.

Cookies are dying, customers can opt out of app tracking, and the era of influencer marketing has shifted the way people buy. Even if you've noticed an uptick in revenue, you've most likely seen acquisition costs go up in the process.

I know this from experience because I've been there myself. The target we are all aiming at is constantly moving. As e-commerce professionals, it is time to shift and expand our focus toward acquiring and keeping customers in order to create consistent, long-term growth. This book shows you how, including an introduction to a tested methodology called Customer Value Optimization (CVO)—the blueprint for amplifying customer lifetime value (CLV) and up-leveling your e-commerce game.

The Importance of Creating Value

The night after my first and last day as a butcher, I realized something that still guides me: I needed to do something with my life, but not in the way my mother envisioned. She equated "doing something" with getting a job and providing for our family. I saw my purpose in a different way: I wanted to create value for other people. If I did not actually create value in my work, I knew that I would never be happy. Every job would become just another butcher shop I was trying to escape.

After my unsuccessful stint as a butcher, I sold books, became an optometrist, brought the internet to an entire neighborhood in Bucharest, founded a marketing and digital agency company, and sold auto insurance, to name just a few of my endeavors. At one point in my journey, I was making 85 euros a month. Three years later, my first small company was making more than $40K in monthly revenue. Then I lost it all and wound up moving back in with my parents. And things have continued to ebb and flow ever since.

At times, I was convinced I had conquered the world. At other times, the more I made, the more costs I had to deal with. In fact, as revenue grew, I watched profits flatten again and again.

Since 2013, I have built Omniconvert, a firm that focuses on web conversions and optimization for clients throughout Europe and the world. Today, we are a team of fifty people with hundreds of clients using our tools, including well-known global brands like Decathlon, Avon, Culture Kings, and Auchan. Every day I remain on the hunt to create value for others and to help companies do the same for their customers.

That's one of the most important lessons that I have gained in my professional life: You have to prioritize the goal of creating value for others and not just making money. If you provide enough value, the money will chase you instead of you chasing it—like a shadow that finds you on a sunny day.

Here's another way to say it: You can't avoid making money if you provide value to the world. This principle is something that many successful startup companies understand and respect. However, things change as companies grow. Once a company is established, they hire and place highly specialized people at the top of the organization. From there, things begin to revolve around revenue targets or earnings before interests, taxes, depreciation, amortization (EBITDA), etc. Before long, these companies only care about the value that they extract from their customers, while leaders prioritize their decisions based on how much profit they will create. In your lifetime, I am sure you have seen how this type of narrow thinking has played out for companies like Nokia, Kodak, Blackberry, and Blockbuster Video, to name a few. What happened to them? In a word, they became self-centric and stopped being customer-centric.

Nowadays, many companies continue to struggle to measure what matters to them and their customers. Often, these struggles come from chaotic reporting, which leads to disconnected departments and random acts of marketing. In addition, many KPIs focus on what the company *gets* rather than what the company *gives.*

There is one North Star Metric that can capture the essence of a company's health: Customer Lifetime Value.

Customer Lifetime Value at a Glance

One way to define Customer Lifetime Value or CLV, as I will refer to it throughout this book, is as the monetary value across the lifetime of a customer relationship, based on the present value of the projected future cash flow that comes from that customer. Yes, it's a bit of a mouthful. To put things simpler, CLV shows you the predicted profit, over time, that a customer will bring you. With this in mind, CLV is the best way to align your entire organization around your customers and to follow the shortest, smartest path to profitability.

Even though CLV has been around for decades, it hasn't been massively adopted by companies. It remains a KPI that data professionals or marketing teams use to adjust budgets or to represent the upper limit on spending to acquire new customers.

This is short-sighted thinking. CLV is actually the ideal KPI to monitor and improve an entire organization's performance. It affects and impacts almost every department, not just marketing, which must work together like an orchestra. What's more, the actions your company takes will affect CLV as a core metric: your products, pricing policy, fulfillment, customer experience, marketing, customer service, and more.

Adding everything together, CLV is a way to monitor performance at every level, starting with the CEO. With the help of CLV, stakeholders can effectively evaluate how well a company's leadership team is doing its job.

And now for a big reveal: Everything changed for my eCommerce business when I began focusing on CLV. After a pivotal a-ha moment, I realized that to improve CLV, my company, and all companies for that matter, must have three solid pillars:

- What they sell (the product)
- What they do (the customer experience)
- What they say (their marketing)

From there, I created the Customer Value Optimization (CVO) methodology, which you are about to discover and start to leverage as you read this book. What you will find is that CVO is the path toward amplifying customer lifetime value.

What Does Value Mean to Your Customers?

The CLV Revolution paints a picture of what value is, why it matters, and how to create it within the context of your business—and, more importantly, in the eyes and minds of your customers. It doesn't stop there. It also gives you direct access to the tools you'll need to use CVO in your business right away.

Here are two truths I'd like to share with you. The first is about the e-commerce landscape and today's businesses. Companies can no longer rely on their old ways. We need an actual revolution—one that begins with a transformed mindset. Congratulations—holding this book is a clear sign that you're on the right path!

Here is the second truth about your customers. They don't buy your product just because of the product. They buy it because they believe your product will make their lives better. They buy it for the job it will perform. They want to improve an aspect of their lives, and something about your product helps them take action.

One reason why an acquisition-only approach will fail is that it doesn't have your customers' unique journeys in mind or how the way they define "value" changes over time. The acquisition-only approach is too busy bombarding people with a stream of "buy-now" messages, offering specials and discounts they might not care about. Plus, the costs of acquisition marketing continue to go up, and you arrive at a sure-to-fail process that all too many e-commerce professionals continue to buy into.

To succeed with a new mindset that moves beyond acquisition only and fills in the e-commerce gaps with lifetime-value marketing, you must become even more customer-centric than before. Across every industry, the shift from acquisition-only marketing to lifecycle marketing is already happening. However, even e-commerce companies that understand the importance of CLV, they're not sure how to achieve it. That's where Customer Value Optimization comes in.

The CVO methodology is a working process that helps e-commerce professionals and businesses deliver value across every stage of the customer's journey: acquisition, onboarding, retention (prevention), and reactivation. CVO helps you understand what this value means to your customers and how your products and services help fulfill their needs again and again, even when those needs change. With this insight, you can begin to deliver greater value via your products, services, and customer support.

Get to Know Your Ideal Customers

I can't tell you all the times I used to think that I already knew my ideal customer before I actually did or that I'd done all of the work I could possibly do to get to know them. I was wrong. If you assume that you've figured your customers out but haven't gathered the data to back up your assumption, the e-commerce world will punch you in the nose. CVO is your chance to go much deeper than just gathering a shallow interpretation of your customers and their needs. With this new insight, you can begin delivering greater value via your messaging and customer support.

To help you gain this insight and put it to use, *The CLV Revolution* unfolds in three parts:

- Part 1 helps you start to fill in the gaps related to acquisition-only marketing, including a deep look at the numbers that drive e-commerce revenue and success. You'll discover that the equation "profits = revenue minus costs" is merely the start, not the end. You will understand why chaotic reporting is the shortest path to disconnected siloes. You'll also see why data hygiene is incredibly important but is far from enough for a thriving data-driven organization.

At the end of part 1, you will see different ways your actions can impact CLV and will understand why it is the North Star Metric to rely on in retail.

- Part 2 expands the CLV message by diving deeper into CVO and providing a practical guide to optimization. You'll learn about customer research and how to move away from fictional buyer personas to real customer expectations. You'll also see how to segment your customers by using RFM and how to take action with the help of real examples from companies that I have worked with. Part 2 reinforces the fact that your customers are at the center of everything. By the end of part 2, you'll be well on your way to getting to know them, understanding why they bought from you the first time, why some continue to buy, and why others have disappeared.
- Part 3 explores six campaign initiatives you can leverage right now with the help of customer data and insights that CVO will help you gain. You may even be tempted to dive into part 3 right away. You can certainly do that, but if you haven't shifted your thinking toward CLV, even the best initiative will fail to deliver the results you want. Sadly, this is actually what almost everyone does right now with their marketing: They throw creative ideas across different channels without knowing at a deep level what triggers customers to buy. It's like being a doctor who starts with a prescription before a diagnosis.

Are You Ready to Change?

If there is only one statement about e-commerce that's true, it's this: e-commerce is always changing. In fact, it's changing right now and will change again in three months and again in a year, no matter what year you are actually reading this. If you're going to survive, you have to be ready to change with e-commerce. Notice I did not use the words "thrive," "excel," or "win." I used "survive" because your survival is tied to your ability and willingness to change your thinking.

The CVO methodology is not something I created overnight. It was forged during hundreds of campaigns for dozens of businesses from around the world. With *The CLV Revolution,* I am bringing these tools to you, so you can put the CVO method to use in order to survive and grow, regardless of global disruptions.

What you'll discover is that CVO is not a "nice to have" but a "must have" in today's business reality. To give you as much support as you need, you'll find that this book delivers on many levels:

- You'll have access to a practical, applicable, tested method that helps you and your business actually move the needle.
- You'll find real-life examples and short case studies from successful businesses that have adopted CVO.
- You'll benefit from a series of downloads, videos, and back-end access to Omniconvert's CVO Academy, where experts from around the world present advanced CVO tactics to support your business success.

This book is not a fairytale or book of stories, though you will find stories throughout. More than anything, this book is a hands-on user's manual. I promise not to waste your time on theory. Rather, I will give you access to tools and principles and help you understand and use them in a step-by-step manner.

My goal is to lift the curtain that separates what you've done in e-commerce up to this point and what you should be ready to do next—assuming you want to get ahead of e-commerce and stay on the bleeding edge.

I have tried my best to distill and share with you insights from my own professional journey. I have been blessed to have access to data from thousands of retailers. Using this insight, I have attempted to bring you essential findings that you can use to change the destiny of your company and become a true pioneer of the CVO method.

If you are willing to stay with the journey and ready to do the work you'll find throughout this book, then you will arrive at the outcome you envision for yourself and your business.

As you'll see, this book cuts to the chase. To start, I'd like to offer this critical piece of insight: The e-commerce equation referred to earlier, which most people follow (profits = revenue minus costs), is incomplete. To go forward, we must unpack this equation and fill in the gaps.

Are you ready?

Let's begin!

PART I

E-Commerce Success Begins with Your Customers

CHAPTER 1

The Path You're Following Is Incomplete

There are tons of books stating that a company's main source of growth comes from the decisions its leaders make. However, according to research by S&P Global, only 26 percent of companies state that nearly all of their decisions are data-driven.[1] If both of these statements are true, then where are nearly three-quarters of leaders getting their information, if not from data?

1 Aslett, Matt: "Delivering Value from Data." 451 Research. https://www.spglobal.com/marketintelligence/en/documents/sp-global-delivering-value-from-data.pdf.

EXTENT OF DATA-DRIVEN DECISION-MAKING

To what extent would you say strategic decisions at your organization are currently 'data-driven'?

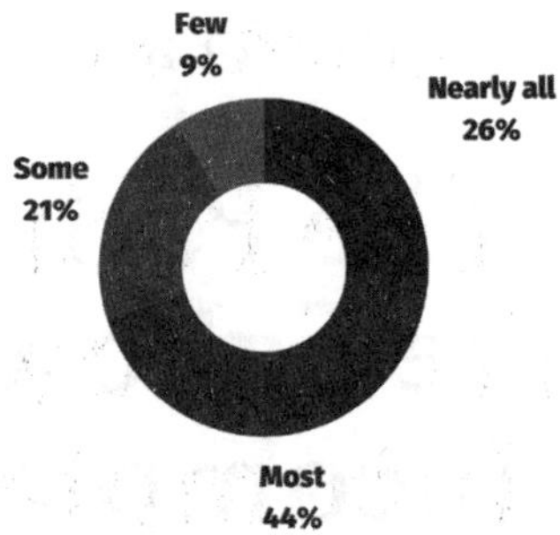

Source: 451 Research's Voice of the Enterprise Data & analytics 2H 2021 S&P Global Market Intelligence

Here is one reason why this is happening. Although most executives understand different ways growth happens and even have data to support their understanding, they can't always convey this important message across their organizations. These leaders get stuck trying to convince everyone else that these things matter. Like everything in business, to gain institutional adoption, you must have critical mass.

Leaders must act as agents of change in order to get other executives on board. Then, they must champion this message across all levels of the organization until enough people understand the rationale and buy-in to support their efforts.

Here is some bad news: Even when the CEO is the agent of change behind an initiative, if the rest of the organization does not align with the decision, adoption will be lacking, and the change will fail to take root.

For something to go from being one person's conviction and become a company-wide mandate, you must have facts, data, and a strong business case that shows why it matters.

Perhaps you find yourself in a similar situation. You are fighting organizational inertia, stuck in the land of chaotic reporting, conflicting KPIs, frustration, and painfully slow progress. It's time to get you out of that mess.

The Change is Already at Your Fingertips

Only a handful of traditional retailers have updated their thinking to leverage the new goldmine that is right at their disposal—customer behavior data. Their unwillingness or inability to change keeps them trapped in an old model that slows innovation, prevents agility, and makes it difficult to pivot toward new profitability. In order to change, they must adopt new ways to understand their customers and redefine their organizational understanding of what success really means.

The true path to discovering these new vistas begins with optimizing the customer journey. When companies do so, it's like hopping on a secret highway that bypasses traffic and gets them to their destination faster than they ever expected.

How Do You Measure Profits?

The simple e-commerce equation that most people use for profits reads like this:

Profits = Revenue - Costs

This equation is too simple to be actionable. Throughout chapter 1, I will unpack the variables (root causes) and fill in the gaps. In the process, I will take a much deeper look at the numbers that actually drive e-commerce revenue and success. First, let's talk about your business.

When things are going well, it can be difficult to pause, peel back layers of data, or spend extra time talking with customers. I know this from experience, especially after seventeen jobs and four businesses. In my early e-commerce days, when I was struggling to break even on my acquisition ad spend, I needed to pull my head out of the weeds and actually go talk with customers. Short of that, I needed to at least learn to put my ear to the data, so I could hear what it was saying. That's when I realized that a lot of what I was doing was wrong.

Whether you are a business owner or an e-commerce professional supporting someone else's business, take this to heart: Your business journey is tied to the journeys of your customers more than you realize. In fact, your business success is more about them than it is about you.

In e-commerce, there is always work to do and plenty of new things to learn. Perhaps you have found the key to actually driving traffic to your website. If so, congratulations. We should all be aiming as high as possible in our businesses. However, if you're aiming for the moon and you're off by even a fraction of a degree, you will miss your mark. Maybe that's why many of us never reach it.

Today's major digital networks and performance agencies have a vested interest. They know that the principles of Customer Value Optimization work in their favor. The more your company spends on ads, the higher your Customer Lifetime Value will be for them since you are their customer. Plus, many performance marketing agencies base their charges on how much you spend, not on how much you gain from the media you buy. This gives them a predictable revenue stream—something retailers do not have. They throw up a loud signal that reads exactly the same as the simple profits equation

I shared above: profits = revenue - costs. Then, they equate this signal with another key message that works to their benefit:

Ads = Revenue & Revenue = Growth

Quite convenient for them, right? Their message to you is clear: If you want to continue to grow your company and become more profitable, you must spend even more money on ads. Why? Because of the following cycle of equations:

ads = eyeballs

eyeballs = visitors

visitors = shoppers

shoppers = revenue

What a tricky cycle we're tumbling around in. They have us believe that as long as we chase after revenue, things will be just fine. Even the metric they use to show us we're successful is all about revenue. It's known as ROAS: Return On Ad Spend. In my opinion, this metric is stupid. For one, attribution is unreliable. Plus, they also measure return by how much revenue you generate.

What happened to profits? Shouldn't we be aiming for profits? In the end, ads ≠ profit, not every time, at least. Still, these conglomerates continue to simplify and amplify their message over and over. But you're smarter than that. You know that even when something plays on repeat over and over, that doesn't mean it's right. Unfortunately, not everyone is that smart.

When enough people believe in the same illusion, it becomes a reality that creates grim scenarios for companies that disregard the real e-commerce growth formula that I'm going to share with you.

Sadly, far too many marketing managers continue to blindly adopt ROAS as the go-to North Star metric. Doing so changes their behavior. It's no longer about making a company profitable or caring about what happens downstream with customers' happiness. Instead, they focus on multiplying their ROAS many times over. They let the number lead the way and leave people out of the equation. In the process, these marketing managers become spending managers.

Adopting a New Way of Thinking About Revenue

In what other areas of your life do you feel there is only one way to do something? Even if you can name a few places where you take finite, absolute positions, my larger point is that business is different from life. In business, the moment you decide that there is only one way to do anything, you have worked yourself into a trap.

Very few things in business work in an absolute way. If you are of the mind that the only way forward for your business is through acquisition marketing alone, especially because that is what the dominant media players are telling you, then now is the time to rethink your position.

Let me repeat something I wrote in the introduction: I am not trying to talk you out of acquisition marketing because it is a key part of business growth and success. Instead, I'm trying to help you enhance your approach in a way that helps you market yourself smarter and in a more targeted fashion, so you can connect with customers who will stay with you for the long haul.

There are many ways to achieve business success, but none is more important than Customer Lifetime Value. There are many dots to connect as you shift your focus toward putting CLV to work for you. Along the way, you will begin to see the link between growing your e-commerce and understanding what customers value.

If you continue to do what everyone else is doing or what major media companies like Google and Meta want you to do, you will continue to swim upstream in a crowded marketplace. You owe it to yourself to do experiments, take calculated risks, and explore other ways to achieve business growth.

During the early days of my own e-commerce journey, the relationship between the customer acquisition cost and Customer Lifetime Value was blurry. It wasn't until my fifth year of being an e-commerce entrepreneur that I finally started to understand things to the point where I could put CLV to use for my own business and eventually for others.

What I realized was quite simple on paper: I was spending too much to acquire customers who were either never going to buy again or were only going to buy sporadically over the next few months before disappearing forever.

E-commerce is much more than an acquisition game and also much more than a conversion game. It's also a retention game with everything to do with customer lifetime value. And it's a game that begins and ends with Customer Value Optimization.

Changing the Growth Equation

(TL;DR: If you're not interested in going too deep into data explanations, I've summed this up for you. You can skip to chapter 2, where I talk about how to improve it.

- *You must move away from simple financial figures that show only the past and adopt customer-centric measures like Customer Lifetime Value and Customer Acquisition Costs.*
- *Without those, you're shooting in the dark, and you will not know who to target, why, and how much to spend to acquire those customers.*

Now, if you're a data geek, please continue to read!)

To have a healthy business, you need profits. From a very simple perspective, the profit equation I shared earlier makes a lot of sense:

It's so clean it's almost beautiful. You take your revenue and subtract costs, end of the story. However, to actually move the needle, you need to analyze things in greater depth. You have to understand which factors matter most because the e-commerce game is much more complex than any simple equation will have you believe.

What you'll find, and what this book presents, is that this equation is far from absolute. It's a starting place that points the way forward. Here's a better example of leaning into when it comes to an e-commerce business model:

IN ECOMMERCE, THIS IS THE COMMON UNDERSTANDING

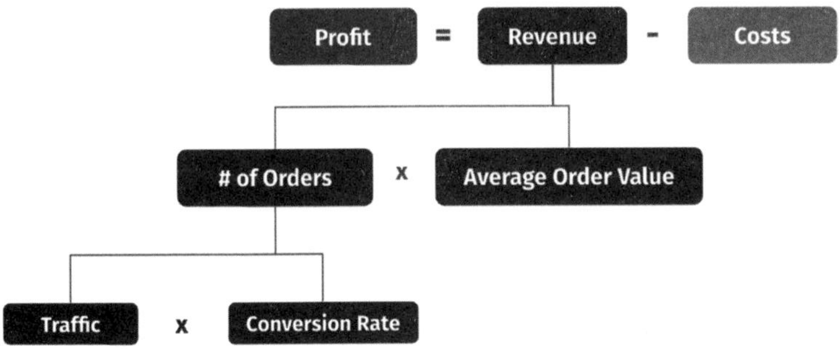

Orders don't just happen out of the blue, right? Actual humans make decisions based on behaviors, desires, needs, etc. New customers choose companies while existing customers return to buy again and again. Depending on the vertical and the maturity of a company, returning customers can generate up to 90 percent of the total revenue.

Here is a picture of aggregated data from my company's benchmarked data, including two thousand e-commerce companies. It shows how the revenue from returning customers grows in importance as a company matures.

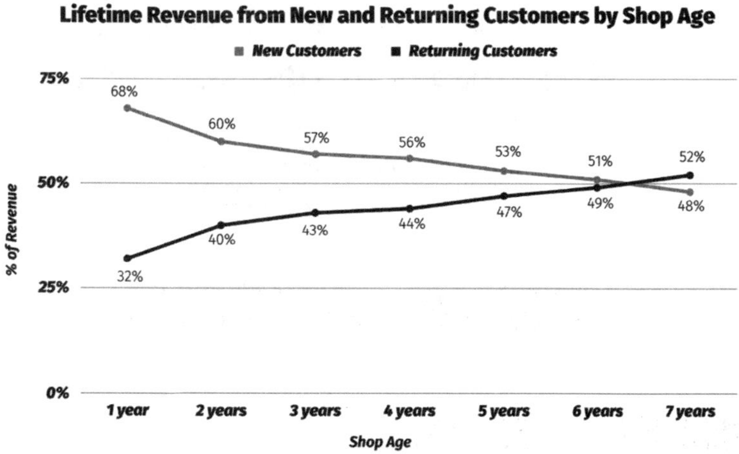

As you can see, the revenue that an e-commerce company generates relies on two streams of revenue: one from new customers and the other from returning ones.

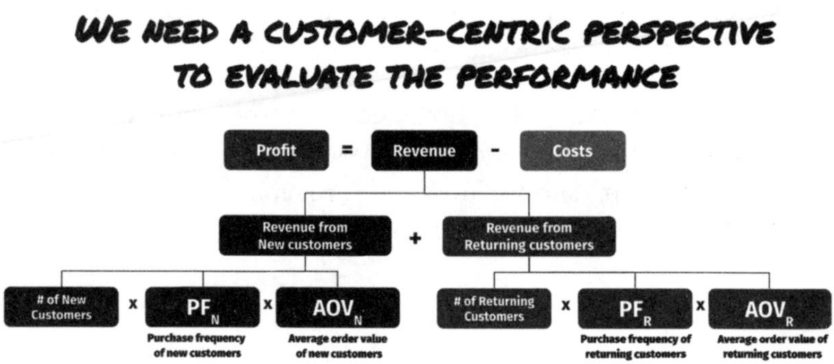

Customer generation comes from a handful of dominant numbers, including the following:

- Traffic
- Average order value (AOV)

- The conversion rate
- Purchase Frequency
- Repeat Purchase Rate

Unpacking the Components of CLV

Before we go too far forward into the land of CLV, I want to unpack some of the less-commonly known terms and components for you. Each of these plays a role in measuring and improving CLV.

Purchase Frequency (PF)

PF represents the number of orders per customer. This number should always be higher than one, as any customer is placing at least one order, and orders are calculated once they are shipped, not just placed.

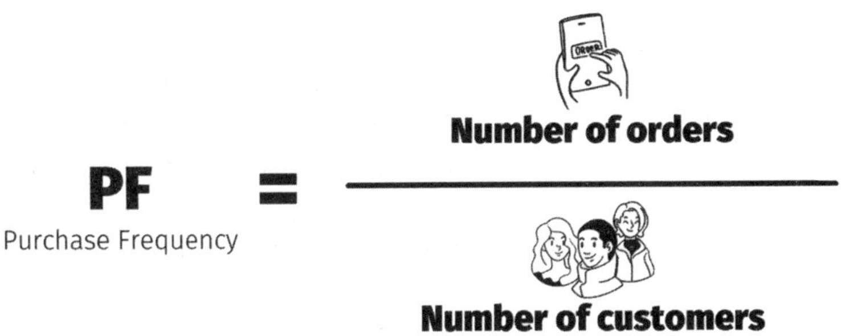

For context, here are some benchmarks with the average lifetime PF by a sample of verticals, which I've borrowed from Omniconvert's data team:

- Food and Drinks: 3.52
- Toys & Hobbies: 2.24

- Apparel: 2.03
- Health: 1.92
- Beauty & Fitness: 1.83
- Home & Garden: 1.53
- Shoes: 1.37

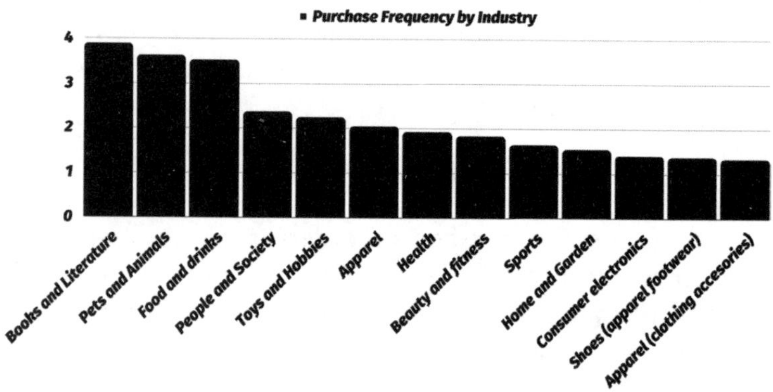

You can use this benchmark to see how your company stacks up against your peers. Keep in mind that these are average figures. For best-in-class companies, their PF might be double the average. Also, remember that "aiming for the average" can be a trap that actually holds you back from achieving your greatest goals. Will see it in chapter 8.

Repeat Purchase Rate (RPR)

RPR is the percentage of customers that are placing at least two orders. However, the issue with this kind of report is that it only gives you data about past performance.

$$\text{RPR} = \frac{\text{Customers with 2+ orders}}{\text{Total Customers}}$$

RPR: Repeat Purchase Rate

In order to pivot toward a brighter future, you need predictive measures you can leverage in ways that help you understand and put the past to work for you in the present. That's one way that Customer Lifetime Value enters the picture. Still, we can't jump into CLV just yet. We need more metrics before we can successfully sort things out.

Customer Retention Rate (CRR)

Often confused with the Repeat Purchase Rate, Customer Retention Rate is one of the most crucial and misunderstood KPIs in all of e-commerce. For example, suppose e-commerce has one-hundred customers at the beginning of an analyzed period. During the period, it acquires one hundred more customers. At the end of the period, they have two hundred actively paying customers. That would be the ultimate dream for any e-commerce business, a customer retention rate of 100 percent!

$$\text{CRR} = \frac{\text{CF} - \text{CN}}{\text{CS}}$$

CRR: Customer Retention Rate

CF: # of customers at the end of period

CN: # of newly acquired customers during the period

CS: # of customers at the beginning of the period

However, if at the end of that period, the number of active customers is only one hundred and twenty-five, that means that the CRR is only 25 percent. This also brings to mind another crucial metric: churn rate.

In this example, where CRR is 25 percent, the churn rate is actually 75 percent. That's not good. In short, CRR measures what percentage of customers continue to buy over a given period. It is the inverse of the churn rate. While churn rate measures the percentage of lost customers, customer retention shows how many you keep. So, when you add these two rates, you will arrive at 100 percent.

Customer Lifespan (CL)

CL refers to the expected time that a customer will remain a paying customer. This is heavily dependent on your business model and how you define churn.

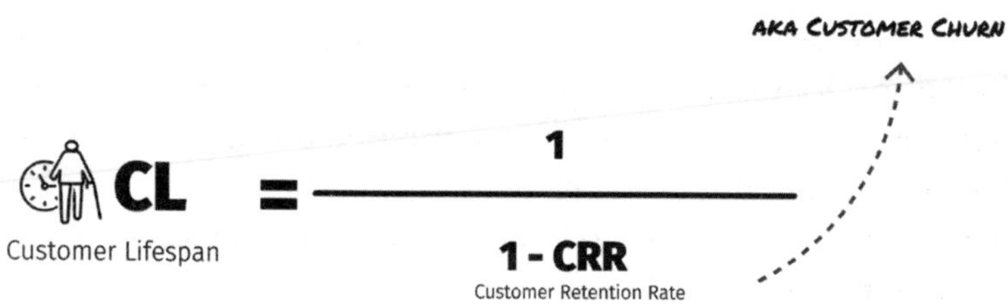

Some would argue that it's impossible to predict when a customer is going to stop buying from you. Believe it or not, there are a number of predictive-type metrics and indicators, including a drop in purchase frequency or a lower net-promoter score. You and I will look deeper into these indicators in part 2.

Gross Margin (GM) and Costs of Goods Sold (COGS)

I've decided to include GM and COGS because they tend to go hand-in-hand in the minds of many business owners. Typically, they include a swarm of other costs related to the following:

- Direct materials
- Direct labor
- Equipment costs involved in the production
- Utilities for the production facility
- Shipping costs

$$\text{GM} = 1 - \frac{\text{COGS}}{\text{Net Revenue}}$$

GM: Gross Margin (%)

COGS: Costs of Goods Sold

**All the terms must be calculated according to the analyzed period*

Let me add three quick notes before we move on.

1. Customer Retention Costs (CRC) can include a number of micro-details, including and related to customer retention, remarketing, emailing campaigns, wages, tools, and more.
2. Not everyone agrees that shipping costs should go into the COGS. Many of my clients include these costs in their thinking, which is why I have decided to include them here.

3. To go deeper into other dominant numbers that impact e-commerce, two other costs to include in your thinking are the cost to produce and ship your products and the costs involved in selling them.

Customer Acquisition Cost (CAC)

One debate when it comes to pinning down an actual formula for Customer Lifetime Value involves whether or not to include Customer Acquisition Costs (CAC). CACs help you see how efficient you are when it comes to acquisitions. For example, when CLV goes down, an understanding of CAC helps you peel back the layers and focus your thinking. Did CLV go down because of acquisition inefficiency? Bad pricing? Low-quality products? Something else?

To be able to monitor these aspects, a more inclusive ratio looks like this: CLV: CAC. This shows how much you're expected to gain from a customer across a lifetime (CLV) vs. how much you paid to acquire that customer in the first place (CAC).

Eventually, you arrive at a much more complete understanding of the dominant numbers that drive the true e-commerce equation.

The most important element to remember is that CAC means much more than what you spend on media to get in front of more eyeballs. This points back to something I wrote earlier in this chapter: you cannot simply pilot your e-commerce plans around ROAS and hope that it flies on its own.

Net Promoter Score (NPS)

Although not part of typical financial metrics, NPS is crucial for measuring customer loyalty and satisfaction. Calculating NPS is fairly simple: You ask customers to rate how likely they are to recommend your product or service on a scale of 0-10. Then, you subtract the percentage of "detractors" (people who give a rating of 0-6) from the percentage of "promoters" (people who give a rating of 9-10).

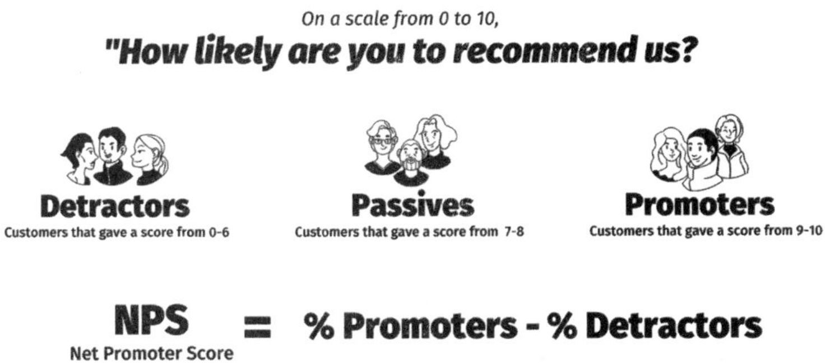

Many businesses have been using NPS for years, and you'll see it pop up throughout this book.

The Customer Lifetime Value Formula

Having gotten a better idea about the numbers that go into CLV, let's take a look at the CLV formula for e-commerce and retail:

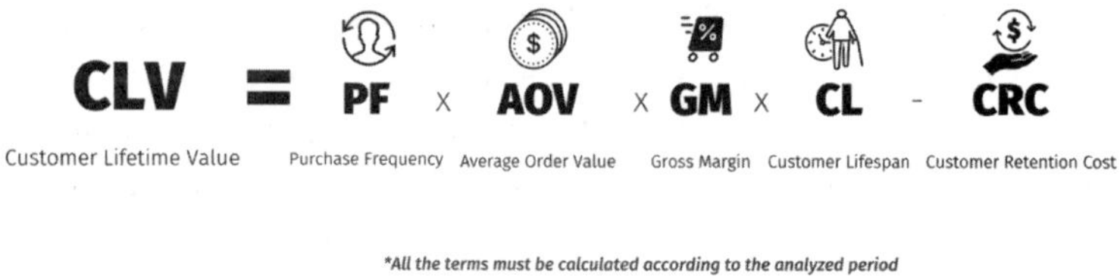

Now, what happens when you need to delve deeper into CLV?

For instance, let's say you need to measure cash flow against marketing spend. Good news—you're on the right track to being able to do so. To illustrate, let's look at a real example. As we do, let's pay close attention to CAC. It's a reminder that CAC, on its own, does not provide enough information to look ahead.

Suppose you're selling beauty products, and you have invested $50 to acquire a customer named Jane Jones. After one year, Ms. Jones made purchases on five different occasions. The total margin that she generates in those purchases comes out to $126.

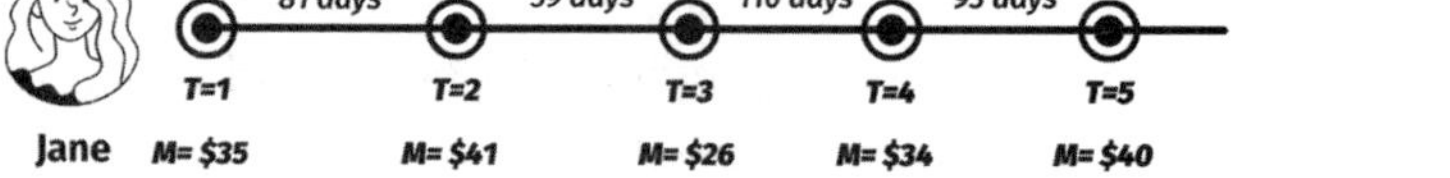

Historical Customer Lifetime Value
(Captured Value - where Gross Margin - CAC = Value) from Jane so far:
M - CAC = (M1 ... M5) = $176 - $50 = $126

If we subtract the CAC from the total margin, we arrive at the margin from Jane's five orders in the following equation:

$35 + $41 + $26 + $34 + $40 - $50 = $126

This represents the captured (historical) CLV, in a model where Value = Gross Margin. Keep in mind that there are multiple models, some of which consider net margin or revenue as the value. I'll continue to use Value = Gross Margin here.

As we look at the data in detail, we start to notice a few things:

- Upon Jane's first purchase ($35), your company was in the hole for $15 (it cost you $50 to acquire her as a customer).
- From there, it took 81 days to break even and gain profit from Jane as a customer.

This measure is called the CAC payback period. It is crucially important in acquisition marketing, as it represents the bridge between finance and marketing. In the end, eventually making money by acquiring customers only works if you have the cash flow you need to support your investments. When the CAC payback period becomes too long or the dropoff becomes too steep, you will eventually go bankrupt.

As it stands, glancing at the information above does not tell us how high Jane's CLV will be. We can only gain that insight if we group her with other similar customers to understand her future purchase probability. Luckily for us, Customer Lifetime Value is a predictive measure, not a historical one.

To calculate CLV, we need to know the customer retention rate, purchase frequency, and margin. In addition, it also helps to look at something called Net Present Value. This includes future discount rates (the cost of capital), which reflect the necessary ROI given the riskiness of future cash flows.

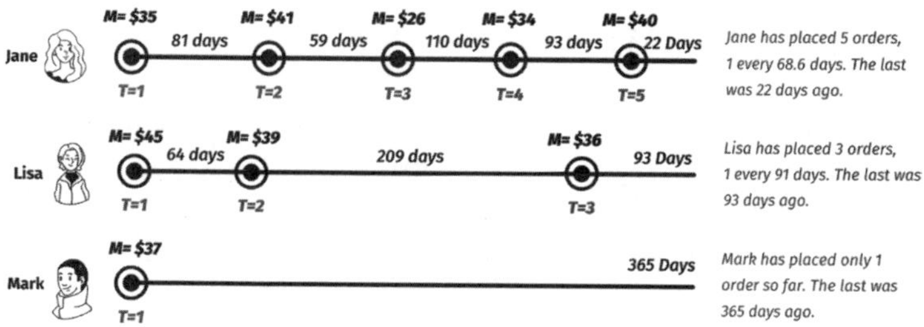

If this store would have only these 3 clients, then the ADBT (Average Days Between Transactions) would be calculated like this: ADBT = 343 + 273 / 8 = 77 days, while the Purchase Frequency (PF) would be like this: PF: 9/3 =3

Once you generate a blended CAC, which aggregates data from multiple customers, a new question comes to mind: How do you know which channels to bet on for marketing purposes? I'll be addressing this question in greater detail throughout parts 2 and 3. For now, I want to point out that there are some leaps of faith you'll need to make, especially considering that nailing any CAC channel is difficult to do.

Needless to say, you and I are just beginning to scratch the surface of things to take into account when your goal is to measure the health of your e-commerce business. Again, my point at this juncture of the book is not to make you dizzy. It's to help you understand the importance of CLV as being a dominant part of how you must think about e-commerce.

The Big Picture

Here are some key thoughts to take with you into chapter 2. First, decades of acquisition marketing have tricked us all into believing that we must spend more to acquire more and that this is the only path toward e-commerce success. We have been told to focus only on net-spend and to look primarily at cost-per-acquisition numbers. As you continue to make your way through *The CLV Revolution*, you will see and understand the much larger picture.

Secondly, what we must chase down and understand as e-commerce professionals is a thorough understanding of the many pieces that contribute to the total customer acquisition cost and cost-per-acquisition. The tools that you will be downloading and using, starting in chapter 2, will help you begin to see what you are really spending per customer.

You will also see that these costs are like a ripple that has many layers to it. Even just a rudimentary breakdown begins to bring a number of things to light, including:

- Costs of goods sold
- Marketing costs
- Salaries and overhead
- Cost of capital

These costs and many others never stop. Combined, they not only add up, but they also determine whether or not you are truly profitable at the end of the day.

Finally, to make your company thrive, you must look at all seven of the dominant numbers I shared a few pages ago. When you begin to move them in one direction or another, you start to understand which ones are the most important for your business at a particular moment in time.

Remember, you can't fight every battle at the same time. You have to pick and choose. In the next chapter, you will begin to pick the CLV battle that makes the most sense to your business right now with the help of CVO. To start, we'll look at how you can impact CLV in your business.

CHAPTER 2

Yes, You Can Impact CLV

Every business wants new ways to generate profits in order to thrive and survive. As I wrote in chapter 1, we must look deeper at how we define the path to achieving profits beyond the simple "revenue minus costs" equation.

Let's evaluate things through the lens of a different equation I shared in chapter 1:

Grouth = actual traffic x conversion rate x ADV

Now let's expand the equation across a customer's entire lifetime:

Grouth = # of Customers x Customer Lifetime Value (CLV)

Keep this in mind as we go forward.

E-commerce Is Still Relatively Young

The earliest e-commerce businesses came about in the 1990s. After the dot-com bust, a handful of successful entities came to dominate the market. Eventually, more and more brick-and-mortar companies launched e-commerce wings. Following the COVID-19 lockdowns, even more e-commerce businesses tried to grab online real estate. Today, almost every business in the e-commerce sphere is starting to see that acquisition-only is not the only way.

Something funny I've heard throughout my career is that it's impossible to impact Customer Lifetime Value. People who say this think of CLV like it's oxygen, an element that exists on its own and can't be changed. I beg to differ.

From Traffic to Customers

Consider your online customers. It's safe to say that they found your website in any number of ways. It could have been one of the following:

- A paid ad
- Word-of-mouth marketing
- An email blast or online newsletter
- Organic search
- A social media share

Ideally, most of your customers will find you via organic search or unpaid promotion. Sadly, our world is far from ideal. Unless your brand has a strong foundation in the hearts and minds of many people, you're probably hustling a bit to win their attention.

No matter how they arrive, you want visitors to proceed to checkout. Then, you want them to come back again and again.

Far too many marketers, e-commerce pros, and business owners stick to the shallow side of the pool when they want to swim around in what drives revenue and profits. The current competitive landscape is forcing some to go deeper and actually hold their breath underwater as they dive into what turns visitors into customers and eventually into customers for life. Guess what's waiting at the bottom of the pool? That's right... CLV.

Customer Lifetime Value is a result of how many customers buy again. It includes a variety of metrics related to retention, purchase frequency, average order value, and gross margin.

Remember the seven dominant numbers graphic from chapter 1? The CLV layer is where more owners and e-commerce operators should be focusing and around which they should be developing clearer goals. The pieces that exist at this layer will actually begin to move the needle.

As you go deeper into the CLV layer, you'll find more and more numbers that influence the ones above. For instance:

- The number of orders and how it affects purchase frequency
- The product return rate
- The average days between days with transactions (ADBT)
- How many orders a customer purchases per month

To beat the CLV drum again now is certainly the time to go deeper than you've gone in the past. And trust me, going deeper is just the start. As you delve into the numbers, you have to know which numbers matter most for your business. You can't lose all of your focus trying to optimize just one or two. So what will it be? Will you...

- Optimize for traffic?
- Optimize for customer conversion rate?
- Optimize for something else?

The list goes on and on.

Changing the Way You Do Business

Decades of acquisition marketing have brought many e-commerce professionals into believing that growth means acquisition and acquisition only. Or, more precisely, it means paid acquisition. To flip this dynamic, we have to diversify channels. But how?

Diversification protects your business from over-relying on only one or two aspects of building growth. Within the dynamic of Customer Lifetime Value, we're looking for ways to diversify beyond customer acquisition and, as a by-product, reduce the costs associated with chasing down acquisitions again and again.

Here are a few things to know about the current state of e-commerce. First, there is a general lack of formal education. This fact actually drove my desire to launch CVO Academy, which is tied to this book.

A second issue relates to the speed of development and investment that large digital media players have woven into their retention strategies. These corporations have found a wrinkle that focuses on educating e-commerce professionals, people like you and me, on how to optimize ad campaigns. These gatekeepers also hold the key to get through the door. They reinforce the need, then offer the solution.

You're smart. You know there's more than one solution. You must pair acquisition efforts with retention. In the end, when you build a strong brand that thrives on word-of-mouth, strong referrals, and a steady stream of repeat business, you spend less on ads.

Getting Customers to Buy Again

It's too expensive to acquire customers that never come back. You need them to come back again and again. To earn their trust, you must make them happy. To earn their referrals and word-of-mouth marketing, you must make them *really* happy. If you keep ignoring their happiness, you're also ignoring your success—and perhaps your survival.

Maybe things are going well for you with your acquisition-first or acquisition-only mindset. If it's not broken, why change it? Well, in my professional estimation—one that many of my contemporaries share—e-commerce as we know it is breaking:

- There is more competition and more demand than ever. The pool you are swimming in is extremely crowded.
- There are more attention-grabbing opportunities that lure eyeballs away from one thing and toward another. Customers have more options than ever before.

This awareness is waking some companies up to the fact that they must optimize more of the touchpoints beyond just two or three dominant numbers. They are showing a willingness to go deeper and avoid the lure of staying with a shallow approach. But notice that I didn't write "most" companies are waking up to this. Only some are. Is your company one of them? Let's make sure it is.

Are You Over-Optimizing For Acquisition?

Ad Networks want you to pay for ads. It costs your customers nothing to use their networks. If Google's only job was to provide the world with free search, they couldn't afford this business model. They need you to buy ad space on their platform, and they're doing a great job convincing you that you need to buy more and more of it to get more and more eyeballs on your website.

There is no danger in this model for them, but there is for you. This is where knowing the right dosage of the acquisition comes into play. Can you actually have too much? Yes. And when it's too much, you endanger your company by over-relying on acquisition or on paid acquisition. Depending on your business model, this scenario can easily happen.

One reason this is happening comes down to old-fashioned organizational inertia. Change is difficult, especially when things seem to be going okay. And when there's a gap in education—when people and companies aren't aware of the entire iceberg—it's easy to fall back on what you know. If there's no one in the organization to question your methodology, then who is going to stop it from happening over and over? Unfortunately, no one will stop it until it stops on its own because you have burned through your acquisition spend, and you have never developed a different approach.

In this type of environment, the definition of the word "marketing" becomes very narrow. It effectively comes to mean "spending money on ads." That's all. Again and again, companies throw money at Google, Meta, and even TikTok and hope for the best. Maybe certain ad campaigns will help lead to short-term gains.

If you have not built a foundation for converting eyeballs into customers and then keeping those customers coming back and spreading the word to others, then the short-term gains will flatten out, and you eventually wind up right back where you were—or worse.

Your spending needs to be about much more than blindly throwing money at acquisition ads. It has to be wrapped up in a learning equation that involves elements such as the following:

- Studying your customers
- Understanding buying habits
- Doing research
- Analyzing post-purchase touchpoints
- Customer journey optimization.

But again, if you are taking a shallow, untargeted, acquisition-only approach, then you are probably not taking these steps.

Defeating Confirmation Bias

I mentioned earlier how e-commerce is a fairly new way of doing business. Today, it remains a moving target. Still, plenty of business owners and professionals feel like they have figured it all out. Now they can sit back and watch the money roll in. I know that's not you because if it were, you wouldn't be reading this book. But just in case you are dealing with someone who possesses this mindset, I want to give you some tips to help you push back.

First, the biggest problem is that when a person locks their thinking in this way, they put themselves and their business in jeopardy of losing everything. The reason: their staunch commitment to their own beliefs makes them inflexible in the face of change.

Despite having more access to data than ever before, many e-commerce owners and professionals continue to make decisions without the help of data beyond the few numbers they have come to trust. In fact, the majority of decisions that most companies make—nearly 74 percent—come from something other than hard data. That means that out of every one hundred decisions a typical company makes, they trust data for only six of them. That's it.

In a world where people turn to data more and more for their own personal decisions, why would e-commerce professionals and business owners not do the same? I can name a few reasons: Stubbornness is one, but so is a general lack of awareness. Many professionals don't know where to turn to find new ideas. Or, they've trusted their guts this far, so why not continue to operate on feelings and hunches? Combined, this points the way to two of the main reasons that many of us have fallen into the acquisition-only trap: 1) a lack of education and 2) a misunderstanding of where to look for help.

There's also the issue of confirmation bias: the Dunning-Kruger effect. It states that the more powerful you are or competent you are in a subject, the less you self-assess. It's easy to stay confident and outspoken, even in areas where you actually lack knowledge on particular subjects. This means you can have no competence at all, but if you rule the roost, so to say, not only will others be reluctant to challenge you, but you will be reluctant to challenge yourself.

I don't mean to knock anyone's success, be it your own or the person who signs your paycheck. But I will say this: Being a successful business owner is different from being a successful e-commerce professional. In my experience, the most successful business owners can recognize when they lack competence or when they need to look for experts to take the reins. In the e-commerce game, this does not always equate. However, the most successful e-commerce professionals know whom to trust and how to use data to their advantage.

Being over-confident in a field where you lack expertise keeps you from assessing and reassessing your perspectives. You wind up jumping from bandwagon to bandwagon, trying to chase down the magical pill. "Let's try this social media platform now. No, let's try that one." And so forth. When you do this, you wind up driving your employees crazy and your company straight into a ditch.

Impacting Your Future with CLV

E-commerce companies that will change have leaders who are willing to learn or are at least willing to let someone else take the lead when it comes to delving into the many nuances that come their way. The most critical aspect of this step is expanding your view of the dominant numbers. Until you start to monitor and measure key metrics related to CLV and build a game plan toward improving them, you will continue to over-optimize the two or three dominant numbers you're used to.

As you keep shooting blindly at a target, you might hit something now and then, but over time, you're setting yourself up to lose. When you begin to pay attention to CLV, you can no longer pretend that your only hope is to aim blindly in the dark. It's time to shine the light you need.

Some marketers think it's impossible to impact CLV. That mindset will only hold you back. The fact is CLV is not a fixed reality. Impacting it is well within your reach if you know where and how to look inside the numbers.

Many companies fail to impact CLV because they monitor it incorrectly or ignore it completely. They want to look at their profit and loss statement (P&L) and then go from there. But here's the thing: Your P&L statement does not show the future, only the past. CLV actually gives you a glimpse into the future. It actually allows you to see if the future looks better or not. So, when you alter CLV, you alter your future.

Lots of e-commerce professionals know what Customer Lifetime Value is in theory and can even explain why it matters. However, if you ask them to describe how CLV aligns with their business or how it has changed in the last three months, many of these people will likely shrug. Why? Because they have not found a way to begin putting CLV to work for them. Yes, they know it exists and why it's important. But they don't know how to apply it, or how to bring it into the fold of their business.

A lack of education may be one reason why people don't attempt to move the needle on CLV, but another is because the tools they are using are severely outdated. I have been under the spell of Google Analytics for a few years, as well, when it came to business metrics and success measurement. It's an easy spell to fall under, especially when the Google machine constantly churns out its acquisition message.

I was wasting my time trying to attribute what the analytics were saying with what my profits and loss statements were showing. I was tracking visitor data and trying to equate it to financial data, but I was ignoring anything that could have pointed the way to better customer insights—items related to finer details and deeper numbers we looked at in chapter 1.

Back then, it wasn't easy to find tools that would help to extract the type of valuable information I needed. And whenever I did find one, they weren't easy to use. In the end, I was wasting my time looking only into Google Analytics, which provided visitor data and financial data, but not customer data.

Of course, you need to see the financial outcomes of your business. But also you need customer data. In business, if you rely too heavily on one data stream but overlook others, you will wind up working with blinders on. Taking this message a step forward, if you rely only on visitor data alone, or even on financial data, you will be spending too much of your attention on lag indicators, which tell you what happened but won't help you shift toward what you want to happen, or help you predict what will happen in the future.

To gain a better view into the future, you need to work with lead indicators, which provide clarity and understanding of what actually causes revenue to happen.

Having the Right Tools and the Right Team

I want to share an important note here about the work of increasing CLV, and continuing the CVO journey. While you can certainly do it alone, it helps to have a team around you. I've learned this from years of experience. Did I go faster on my own? Yes. Did I go farther with my team? Absolutely. I believe that you will go farther, too, with some help, including in areas where you may not be an expert. For instance:

- A writer or content creator for the great creative you'll be producing.
- Data analyst to dig deeper into the numbers.
- A marketing expert who can sync up the creative and the data in the smartest way possible and manage your media team, email endeavors, ad buys, etc.
- Consumer insight professional (CRM lead).
- Technology ally or a software architect who can implement various tools.

If you don't have these people at the ready, consider working with an agency or team of specialists as you move forward.

Our CVO Academy program is a good example. You'll have insider access to the academy as you continue this book. Moreover, we have already trained a few CVO agencies that you can decide to work with.

The E-commerce Growth Formula

The metrics that show how and why profit happens to go far beyond the number of visitors who come to your e-commerce site. Uncovering them begins when you dig deeper into actual customer behavior.

Here's a snapshot visual of the growth formula:

eCommerce Growth Formula

KPIs	Initial status	Uplift	Best case scenario (everything +20%)	What-if scenario (+20% traffic)	What-if scenario (+20% conversion rate)	What-if scenario (+20% PF)	What-if scenario (+20% AOV)	What-if scenario (-20% CAC)	What-if scenario (+20% Margin)
Traffic	1,243,322	20%	1,491,986	1,491,986	1,243,322	1,243,322	1,243,322	1,243,322	1,243,322
Conversion rate	1.78%	20%	2.13%	1.78%	2.13%	1.78%	1.78%	1.78%	1.78%
Total Customers	32360		42092	36784	36784	32360	32360	32360	32360
Newly acquired Customers	22118		31,850	26,542	26,542	22,118	22,118	22,118	22,118
Existing customers	10242		10242	10242	10242	10242	10242	10242	10242
PF (Purchase Frequency)	1.11	20%	1.33	1.11	1.11	1.33	1.1	1.1	1.1
AOV (Average Order Value)	$65	20%	$78	$65	$65	$65	$78	$65	$65
Initial Revenue (Customers x AOV x PF)	$2,324,357		$4,353,671	$2,642,096	$2,642,096	$2,789,229	$2,789,229	$2,324,357	$2,324,357
CAC (Customer Acquisition Cost)	$18	20%	$14.40	$18	$18	$18	$18	$14	$18
Projected Revenue per Cohort	$2,417,332		$4,527,818	$2,747,780	$2,747,780	$2,900,798	$2,900,798	$2,417,332	$2,417,332
Gross Margin	52%	20%	62%	52%	52%	52%	52%	52%	62%
Projected Gross Margin per Cohort	$1,257,012		$2,219,235	$1,428,846	$1,428,846	$1,508,415	$1,508,415	$1,257,012	$1,508,415
Revenue uplift			87%	14%	14%	20%	20%	0%	0%
Gross Margin uplift			77%	14%	14%	20%	20%	0%	20%
CLV (RpC)	$80		$138	$80	$80	$115	$96	$80	$80
CLV (including CAC & margin)	$23		$72	$23	$23	$42	$32	$27	$32
CLV / CAC	1.30		4.97	1.30	1.30	2.32	1.76	1.88	1.76
Total Customer Acquisition Cost	$398,124		$458,639	$477,749	$477,749	$398,124	$398,124	$318,499	$398,124
Projected Net Margin per Cohort	$858,888		$1,760,596	$951,097	$951,097	$1,110,291	$1,110,291	$938,513	$1,110,291
Net Margin Uplift			104.99%	10.74%	10.74%	29.27%	29.27%	9.27%	29.27%

Now it's time to put it to use for yourself. Go to the following URL:

BIT.LY/eCommerceGrowthFormula

There are many "e-comm gurus" who argue that you only need to uplift retention by 5 percent in order to realize a 25 percent jump in profits. This type of message might help them generate clicks and likes, but it's the type of advice that doesn't get into the specifics of your business, not to mention your actual numbers.

Accuracy and ease are two of the main features of this tool. In fact, all of the tools you'll download and use as part of the CVO Academy component of this book promise the same: They help you gain an accurate view and are extremely easy to use.

Let's walk through this tool together.

- With the download open on your screen, you can begin to see what happens if you increase or decrease various numbers.
- This is key, and as you continue with this book, you'll be able to apply for your own business numbers in order to gain an accurate picture of where you'll need to focus.

As I said earlier, in some cases, the acquisition may be what you need, and it might still make sense to apply more of your marketing budget toward acquisition. Even when the acquisition makes the most sense for your business needs, the rest of this book will help you target your acquisition messages in direct and powerful ways.

Working with your download, we'll start by looking at what happens when you increase customer retention by 10 percent.

In chapter 1, I discussed how it's important to take a broad view of the dominant numbers that matter most in e-commerce. You'll see those same dominant numbers listed in the left-hand column, along with others. For instance: traffic, conversion rate, and purchase frequency.

- You can view these numbers according to any time frame you choose, such as during the last year, the last quarter, the last month, and so on.
- As you adjust, you can insert average order value, customer retention rate, customer acquisition costs, gross margin, and other key numbers that help you derive a better understanding of your profits over time.
- As you continue to add and adjust your numbers, you can see how a change in this or that column will begin to affect your projected revenue.

You can begin to see what happens if every customer places three orders. Now, assuming this is an ideal ratio for you to create the revenue you need, what happens if only 12 percent of your customers return to place a second order? And, of the 12 percent who come back a second time, what if only 10 percent of them come back to place a third? Here, you begin to see how the margin drops dramatically, which opens up a number of new lines of questioning:

- Do we need to acquire more customers?
- Or do we need to nurture the customers we have in order to extend their lifetime value?

With these questions in mind, you can begin to adjust your numbers in the chart and gain a clearer view of your ideal projections. Let's do some adjustments to the numbers that currently exist in the download:

Let's insert an uplift of 20 percent across the board, to show you the impact of what happens if each of these numbers increases by 20 percent. That means you increase traffic, conversion rate, purchase frequency, and so on by the same amount. However, you'll also increase associated costs by 20 percent, which means acquisition costs go up as well.

Maybe this would be a lot of work for your company, or maybe not—only you know for sure. The main point is to see how an increase of 20 percent across the board will eventually impact your margin on the revenue.

Now, instead of a 20 percent increase across the board, what happens if you increase only the customer lifetime value by 20 percent? How does this impact margin? The uplifting conversion rate changes in your favor because it does not lead to a dramatic uplift in terms of acquisition costs. In fact, the margin impact is four times higher.

Having fun with pretend numbers will only take us so far. It's time for you to set the book down for a bit and begin plugging in your own numbers.

Homework: Fill in the Download with Your Numbers

You don't have to fill in your actual numbers to gain insight from this book. However, it will help you gain an accurate look at what your business actually needs right now.

Perhaps you will determine that acquisition is still the area where you need to put most of your attention. That's fine, and it's good to come to that conclusion now because the chapters that follow will help you be more targeted than ever before in your acquisition messages.

I'd like to remind you of something that you probably already know, whether or not you are thinking about it right now: Life and business are about much more than numbers. They are rich in stories and filled with people. Some of those people are your customers, while others may become customers in the future.

Part 2 of this book is about getting to know your customers. What do they care about? What do they need? How do your products or services make their lives better? Let's answer these questions and many others!

PART 2

Customer Value Optimization: What It Is, and How to Use It

CHAPTER 3

The Power of Customer Value Optimization

By now, you are gaining a stronger understanding of what Customer Lifetime Value is and the ways that you can actually impact it. Sticking with how we ended chapter 2, and assuming you've done your homework, perhaps you have determined that, yes, the acquisition is still the most important direction for you to go. That's a great understanding to come to, and it will help you get even more out of this book.

Starting in chapter 3 and throughout the chapters that follow, the goal of this book is to help you acquire the *right* customers: the ones who will stick around, and with whom you will enjoy long-lasting relationships. Acquisition marketing may have gotten you to where you're at, but it won't help you go forward on its own. Customer Value Optimization (CVO) is the path to creating a great customer journey and amplifying the long-term growth and success of your business.

Understanding CVO

Customer Value Optimization is the process for long-term business health and growth. It focuses on optimization throughout the customer lifecycle to improve brand and customer loyalty. It helps to turn those first-time shoppers into customers you retain for the long term.

To understand how CVO works, we have to first understand the gap between what value means for a customer and for a company. When a company acquires a new customer, it makes money, and it also gets the opportunity to bring more customers through word of mouth, which will eventually lead to more money, as well.

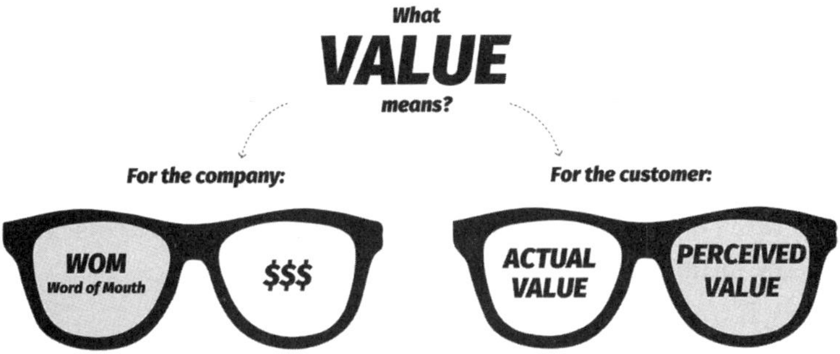

Here's the catch. In such a competitive market, where consumers have myriad of alternatives to buy products similar to the ones you're selling, you have to deeply understand the lenses they see through when they buy. Besides the actual value, there's also the perceived value, which has a tremendous impact on a customer's future actions. That's why companies can't ignore the perceived value their customers apply and bring to the buying experience.

I recently had a brilliant conversation about this on a podcast episode ("CVO Live," if you are inclined) with Bryan Eisenberg. Bryan is a fantastic speaker and author. He contributed immensely to the entire optimization space. He and his brother Jeffrey basically started the conversion rate optimization (CRO) movement.

Bryan helped me understand the gap between how companies see themselves and how their customers see them. It turns out 80 percent of companies think they are customer-centric, but only 8 percent of customers agree.

The story he shared with me began in the state of Texas, USA, where he lived. It was extremely hot, and his air conditioning wouldn't start. The batteries from the AC remote control were fried. He was working from home, and he needed to work in a comfortable setting, not a sauna. He had to buy a $5 set of batteries from Amazon to get them as fast as possible. To qualify for same-day delivery, he needed to spend another $35. He spent seven times more just so he could get the batteries on the same day as his purchase. Funny thing: When the package arrived, the batteries were missing!

Here are some interesting takeaways:

1. For Bryan, the need for the batteries was much higher than their actual surface-level cost. He was willing to spend $40 to get something worth $5.
2. In the process of *not* getting the batteries, the value of Amazon as a company dropped significantly in Bryan's mind.

To understand and improve the value of your company in the eyes of the market, you must understand and optimize the entire customer journey. That process is called Customer Value Optimization.

The CVO Methodology

CVO breaks down into three pillars that influence Customer Lifetime Value (the same pillars I shared in the introduction):

1. What you say (marketing, pre- and post-purchase)
2. What you're selling (the quality of your products matters)
3. What you do (how you behave and how you support the customer journey over time)

Each pillar can be a starting place for the complete CVO methodology, which includes a sequence of steps that I will walk you through as we continue. The list that follows may seem long at first glance, but don't worry. We have already begun to cover some of this ground, and the rest will flow seamlessly in the chapters that follow:

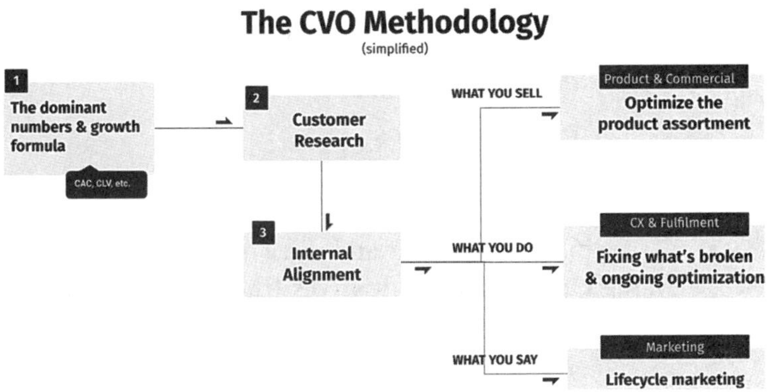

- Monitoring what matters (which I've covered since chapter 1)
- Prioritizing your CVO-related activities
- Gaining insights from Recency, Frequency, and Monetary value (RFM segmentation)
- Running qualitative research
    - Net promoter scores (NPS)
    - Online surveys
    - Jobs to be done interviews
- Quantitative research
    - Validate statistically the insights gathered through qualitative research
- Studying the buying patterns

- Understanding the ideal customer profiles (ICPs)
- Putting ICP insights to work
- Customer journey mapping
- Fixing what's broken in the following areas:
    - Customer service
    - Optimizing products
    - Eliminating frictions
- Building your customer retention strategy
- Using insights to define and run a number of Customer Value Optimization initiatives (the focus of part 3 of this book):
    - Acquisition
    - Onboarding
    - Prevention
    - Referral
    - Loyalty
    - Reactivation

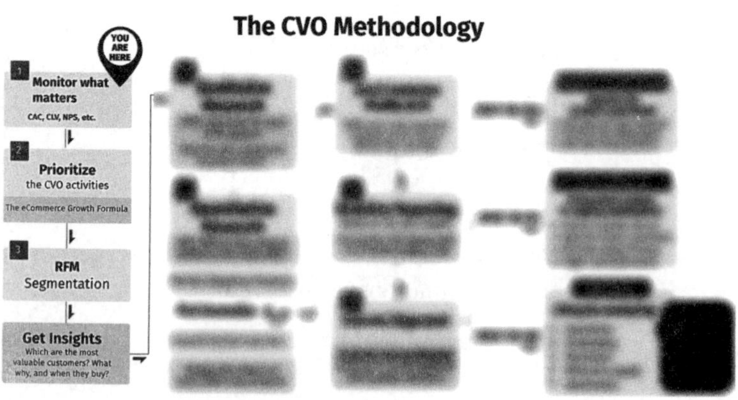

Together, you and I will continue to unpack these steps. At the moment, let's discuss what it means to monitor what matters.

Is Traffic Always Traffic?

If you put all of your energy toward generating more and more traffic but not enough focus on generating the right kind of traffic, then you're not solving anything—you're just bringing more eyeballs to your site without converting them into customers. Sure, you may hit upon an occasional short-term fix, but it will be like plugging up a hole in the side of your house with duct tape. Eventually, the tape will stop working, and you'll be back where you were.

To acquire the right customers, you need to follow through on conducting the right type of customer research. We'll spend more time discussing research in chapters 5 and 6, particularly customer research. However, I want to start the conversation now with an eye toward delving deeply into your own traffic data. To do so, I'd like to share the story that led me to understand the importance of Customer Lifetime Value and on the path to creating the CVO methodology.

When Growth and Churn Collide

The client was a major retailer with brick-and-mortar stores in eleven countries across Europe and a growing online presence. They did their in-house marketing, including studio product photography. From the outside, they had everything working for them.

Revenue growth? Absolutely. They were doubling their business year over year! Their CFO was thrilled about how things were going. However, when I looked more in-depth, I noticed that their customer retention rate dropped by

20 percent year after year, quite an aggressive churn. Meanwhile, their Net Promoter Score (NPS) was lower than 40. Recall that NPS is a key metric when you are trying to enhance customer lifetime value and prevent customer churn. A Net Promoter Score of 40 definitely needs improvement. As a rule of thumb, your NPS score should be above 80, with a 10 percent response rate when reaching out to customers.

They hired us for conversion rate optimization, to help them deal with the high CAC. As revenue grew, their acquisition costs were also skyrocketing. Something had to give. Their team of 15 PPC experts were basically monitoring things from a financial and paid acquisition perspective, looking at Cost-Per Acquisitions, instead of the CLV to CAC ratio or the CAC Payback periods (from chapter 1).

Their main KPI was ROAS (Return on Ad Spend). Personally, I think ROAS is a stupid metric. It shows a skewed perspective of how effective ads are, usually by using a broken attribution model, but neglects gross margin and future purchases from the customers.

Once we started customer research, we realized that in order to improve the conversion rate, the company needed to do one of two things: 1) acquire new customers or 2) entice existing customers to buy again. Their core issue did not involve acquisition and conversion, but retention. They'd fallen into a common e-commerce trap: treating conversion rate as a metric that only showed how well they were doing at acquiring new customers. They needed to shift their focus on how good (or bad) they were at retaining existing customers.

Why weren't their customers coming back? We conducted an RFM segmentation analysis to look deeper. RFM stands for Recency, Frequency, and the Monetary value of each purchase. (If you are not yet familiar with RFM, you will be soon enough. It is a crucial step when your goal is to improve Customer Lifetime Value in retail, and I will begin unpacking it in detail in chapter 4.)

RFM gives you ways to group customers into different segments based on a scoring model that accounts for the following:

- How recently they bought
- How frequently they bought
- How much they spent so far

Notice how the acronym is spelled out: R, then F, then M. Of the three metrics, Recency is the most important, Frequency the second most important, and Monetary spend the third. In many ways, this is the beginning of the work you'll be doing as you get closer and closer to identifying your ideal customers.

As part of the RFM segmentation, we also began to analyze their NPS score, using a handful of micro-factors, including a number of individual product categories. At this point, a deeper story began to emerge from the data, and it wasn't positive. Their products were far from making their customers happy. Their marketing was great, their stores were inviting, and even their customer service earned good scores. But the quality of their products ranked as far down on the charts as you could possibly imagine.

Marketing Does Not Fix a Broken Product

You can't market your way out of a product problem. If you try, it will actually send negative ripples through everything else you want to do as a business. In the case of this company, customers felt frustrated and duped since the company had such slick marketing and branding. How could their products be so bad? This created a vicious cycle from which the company could not escape, no matter how much money they threw at acquisition marketing and paid ads:

- With frequent customer complaints, they were dragging down their customer support operations. For one, the work itself was unhappy. And secondly, the customer service representatives were doing everything they could to get the messages they were hearing up the chain, but sadly, no one up the chain wanted to listen.
- Strangely enough, product returns were not a nightmare. Their products were not expensive, and customers were so frustrated that they didn't even bother sending the products back. They wanted nothing to do with this company ever again.
- The poor reputation of their products had spilled into negative online chatter and bad reviews, which were causing irreparable damage to their brand's reputation.

When we presented the data, they were reluctant to do anything at first. They'd already decided that their issue was conversion and were unwilling to free themselves from this mindset. They were under the spell of confirmation bias. Luckily, a small group from their leadership team had been quietly wondering about the customer issue. Once we shared our data, this group got a little louder.

They eventually shifted gears, but since they couldn't fix their products, no amount of promises or improvements to their CX could fix what was broken. Maybe they could have kept going if their acquisition costs hadn't gotten so large. However, these costs went up astronomically, especially as their market sector and competition became more concentrated. They kept dumping resources toward what they knew, acquisition-focused ads on Google and Facebook. Before our work was finished, they were spending more than $300,000 a month on Facebook ads alone.

By the time the company's leadership made clear that their new North Star Metric will be Customer Lifetime Value, their reputation had already been dragged through the mud. It was nearly impossible for them to source better products because of cash flow challenges. We tried to redirect them, but bankruptcy soon followed. It was a sad demise. Only one of their markets was still standing two years later, then turned out the lights for good.

Trusting Customer Metrics

In many ways, your customers know more about your products and your business than you do. If that's a radical idea, so be it. If you disagree, track me down on LinkedIn and share your thoughts. I'm happy to engage in this conversation.

If you overlook customer metrics, you will fall prey to confirmation bias, just like the company in the story I just shared. You can think you are doing great, and the shallow numbers may validate this thought. On your way to digging deeper, one of the first stops you'll make is at the pile of free insights your customers share every day. They write it in reviews, share it with customer service reps, and post it on social media every time they @ or # your business.

If you point your eyes and ears in the direction of your customers, they will answer the most important questions you can ask, such as:

- Why are they not coming back?
- Why are we dealing with so much churn?
- Why are our acquisition costs going up and up each month?

My client was slow to see and hear the data, and they died a fiery death. For my business, the experience opened our eyes to the power of CLV. It built the foundation for CVO, and showed us how important the following were:

- RFM segmentation
- Net Promoter Score
- Customer experience (CX)
- Knowing why churn and burn are happening
- Listening to data from new sources (CX, for instance)
- Fixing a broken product before too late

As you and I continue this journey, we're going to unravel the mystery of *your* products and services and start looking at them from the standpoint of your customers. Here's why: Even if you sell apples, your customers may be buying something else from you. In fact, here are just four things they're *actually* buying when they buy your apples:

- A burst of energy, packed with vitamins.
- Dental support they pack in their child's lunch.
- Something to enjoy before their jog.
- The core ingredient for their holiday pie.

No matter what you sell, it is just a part of a much bigger solution. Bob Moesta, a mentor of mine, likes to say that your product is not the sandwich but the mustard. For your customers, their life is the sandwich; your product is just one of many ingredients.

As I wrap up chapter 3, I want to point out that you may have already been using elements of CVO without knowing that you're doing so. In the next few chapters, you'll gain a more detailed understanding of all the components, and will be ready to jump into the campaign initiatives in part 3.

I hope that many dots are starting to connect for you between what hasn't been working and what needs to change in your business. Let's take a deeper look at your customer and delve into the wonderful world of RFM segmentation.

CHAPTER 4

Know Your Customers

Not all customers are created equal. In this chapter, we'll start unfolding the first part of the customer research: RFM segmentation. This is the same methodology that big retailers use. It's time for you to put it to work for your business.

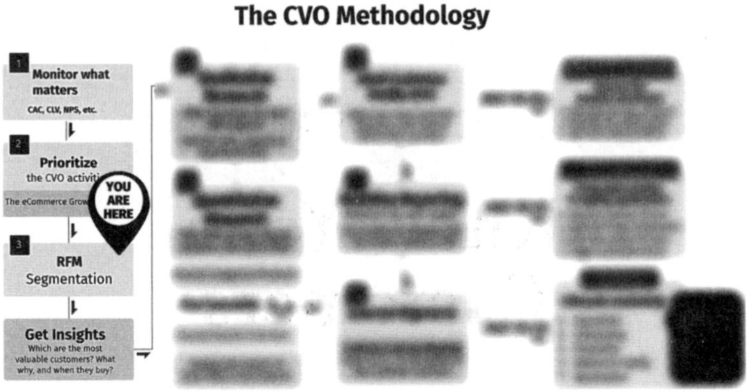

Recency, Frequency, and Monetary Value (RFM)

RFM is the next step toward unlocking the deeper truths about your customers: who they are, why they buy, and what matters to them. With RFM in your arsenal, you will be on your way to uncovering the stories that customer data and insights are trying to tell you. Then, you can shift your messaging to attract and retain more ideal customers.

direct mail marketers were looking for a way to cut printing and postage costs and target their mailers. When they began segmenting their customers by Recency, Frequency, and Monetary spending, RFM was born, with Recency being its most important attribute.

How many thoughts do people have in a single day? Dr. Fred Luskin of Stanford University once found that we have as many as 60,000 thoughts in a day and that the vast majority are repetitive[2]. As time passes, it's less and less likely for someone to remember or act on a single idea. This reinforces why Recency is the most important piece of RFM.

Today, issues related to print and postage spend aren't as extreme as they were in the 1970s. Certainly, many companies and business types continue to use mailers, but by and large, e-commerce professionals are thinking digitally and electronically when it comes to communication. Still, RFM matters and will continue to matter well into the future.

RFM segmentation is an early and smart way to get to know your customers, so you can make sure you're relevant in their minds. But it does something else as well. It tells you why you're important in their minds. And with this information, you can spend your ad dollars in smarter ways. Here are two key points specific to your business to keep in mind as we go deeper into RFM:

- Using RFM is the first step to moving away from "one-size fits all" acquisition campaigns.
- RFM also helps you begin to build stronger and more relevant relationships with different customer types.

---

2 Comaford, Christine. "Got Inner Peace? 5 Ways to Get It Now." Forbes. Forbes Magazine, November 7, 2013. https://www.forbes.com/sites/christinecomaford/2012/04/04/gotinner-peace-5-ways-to-get-it-now/?sh=54c8ac456672

In a few pages, you'll be downloading CVO Academy's RFM segmentation tool. With this tool, you'll have a new way to analyze and segment your customers based on RFM value scores. Before we get there, let's go back a bit and explore what you currently know—and don't know—about your customers.

How Well Do You Know Your Customers?

Do you know why people shop with you? Why do they come back? Or why don't they come back? And before you answer any of these questions, what criteria are you using to back up your answers: data or hunch?

To help you answer these questions, let's use the same methodology that large, global retailers use to find their own answers. Let's also be mindful of what I wrote above—not all customers are created equal. You have to answer the following:

- Who are your best customers?
- What and why do they buy?
- What context led them to consider buying from your store?
- What makes them come back and buy again?
- Can you treat all of them the same way?

At the end of the day, your customers will fall into a variety of categories. To get us started in a very simple way, I will break things down into four segments, using recency and monetary values only. Keep in mind that high and low recency will split customers into two groups: active and inactive. And, since high and low monetary values lead to having low-value and high-value customers, blending them together leaves us with these 4 segments:

- Low-value lost customers
- High-value lost customers
- Low-value active customers
- High-value active customers

Simple, right? Maybe not. Don't worry, you're doing great. Let's keep going.

How to Score

This type of segmentation can work for small companies, where Frequency is not as important. If you sell one-time products, like wedding rings or mattresses, you can use this model (as long as the divorce rate is not enormous in your market). For larger companies or businesses that sell the types of consumable products that keep people coming back (health and beauty, nutrition, hygiene, etc.), we have to complicate things a little bit. Ignoring Frequency and having only two tiers of customers (active/inactive and high-value/low-value, based on Recency and Monetary spend) is not enough. For instance, when can you say that a customer turned from active to inactive? Have you defined this parameter?

To gain an accurate distribution of customers, many larger companies complete RFM analysis using a scale from **1 to 6** to score their customers. That doesn't mean that you need to use this scale. A lot of this comes down to the size of your customer base. Perhaps a scale of **1 to 3** is better for your situation. As with everything you do, the parameters you set must align with the truth of your business, not with some rigid rule.

If you run an online grocery outlet or a marketplace where people shop for household items, your recency and frequency models will be much different than if you sell high-end furniture that people buy once every few years. This is another reason why it's important to model with your actual numbers based on the reality of your business, as well as shopping habits and norms.

You may want to use a larger scale to capture more granular differences between customers. To decide how big the scale should be, you have to be aware of the purpose of the segmentation. If you want to use it as an evergreen way to address customers in the future, make sure you don't end up with too many segments. Otherwise, this will make it more difficult for you to address customers differently down the road. If you just want to analyze customer behavior as a one-off exercise, you can go more granular. This will also help you identify and understand outliers.

Now let's look at a real-world example. Below I've included numbers from a European fashion retailer with a total customer base of roughly 110,800. To work with these numbers, I am going to use a scale from **1 to 4**.

Thanks to all the struggles and the tedious SQL queries that my team and I have been through in the past, I've built the Omniconvert tool so it can adjust the scale and scores automatically or manually from the UI. This makes it easier for users to compare the differences and to decide which model is the best, as you can see below:

	Recency (days)					Frequency (orders)					Monetary (EUR)				
	Range	Customers	€	€ / customer		Range	Customers	€	€ / customer		Range	Customers	€	€ / customer	
1	303 –	75.7K	16.3M	215.3	1	1 – 1	81.4K	13.1M	160.5		0.00 – 105.80	27.7K	1.9M	69.6	
2	137 – 302	11.5K	3.6M	311.8	2	2 – 2	17.3K	5.8M	336.4		105.81 – 165.90	27.7K	3.8M	136.5	
3	43 – 136	12.8K	4.7M	368.6	3	3 – 3	6.1K	3.2M	526.9		165.91 – 290.00	27.7K	6M	215.2	
4	0 – 42	11.1K	4.4M	395.2			6.3K	6.9M	1.1K		290.01	27.7K	17.3M	623.5	

There are 6.3K customers with Frequency (orders) between 4 and ∞

Setting Your RFM Scores

Let's start with setting Monetary points. To do so, I'll use equal percentiles. This is a more accurate way to reflect the distribution of values in your customer base.

- Before you set your monetary value scores using equal percentiles, sort your customer data by monetary value (the amount each customer has spent).
- Then, divide the customer list into equal percentiles (top 25 percent, next 25 percent, etc.).
- From there, assign a monetary value score to each percentile based on the rank of the percentile. For instance, the top percentile gets a score of 4 points, the next percentile gets a score of 3 points, and so on.

In the example above, the groups for the monetary values are equal in size, each with 27,700 customers. Likewise, the customer list lines up equally as well, with each percentile representing 25 percent of the customer base.

As we turn to Frequency points, things get a little tougher. For one, I can't use percentiles so easily to demonstrate frequency. That's because, for most non-contractual businesses, the majority of customers place a single order. Consider this example, for instance:

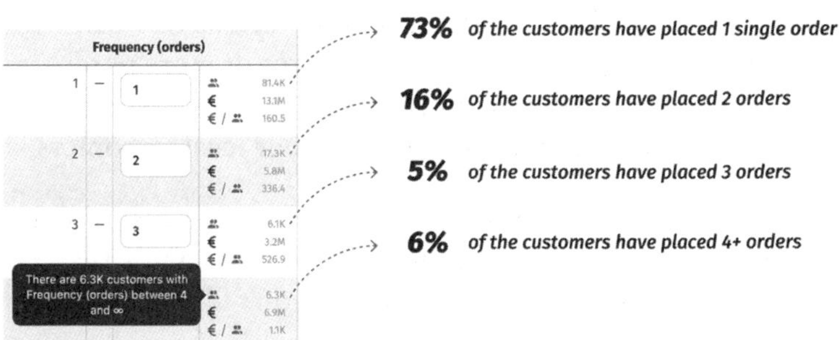

How can we work with this? Well, we can use what I'll call "conscious trade-offs," a tactic that keeps plenty of marriages going. All kidding aside, the idea of conscious trade-offs refers to a series of alternatives, along with a series of consequences.

Here is a simple scale to help illustrate the point: one-time (1), repeat (2+). Using this scale, you can group customers who have made one purchase into the "one-time" category and those who have made two or more purchases into the "repeat" category.

Using this approach gives you **eight** clusters of customers: two scores each for recency, frequency, and monetary (2 x 2 x 2). To break things down, your potential scoring categories look like this:

- 1, 1, 1
- 1, 1, 2
- 1, 2, 1
- 1, 2, 2
- 2, 1, 1
- 2, 1, 2
- 2, 2, 1
- 2, 2, 2

Here's a method that will give you more details to work with later: one-time (1), two purchases (2), three or more purchases (3+). While this gives you more to deal with, it also provides a stronger way to distinguish and find your ideal customers.

When you apply a "three or more" layer across recency, frequency, and monetary spend, you wind up with twenty-seven potential groups of customers. I won't fill the page with bullet points this time, but the basic equation is 3 x 3 x 3 = 27, potential customer groups.

To repeat the broken record again, depending on the truth of your business, you can continue to segment customer groups using larger and larger numbers. For instance:

- one-time (1)
- two purchases (2)
- three purchases (3)
- four or more (4+)

This would give you 64 potential clusters (4 x 4 x 4). And on and on. Again, one of the benefits of having more and more groups is that it can help you distinguish some of the finer details that exist in customers' purchasing habits. For example, what is the monetary impact when a customer makes three purchases, vs. making four or more? How do these additional purchases impact your CAC?

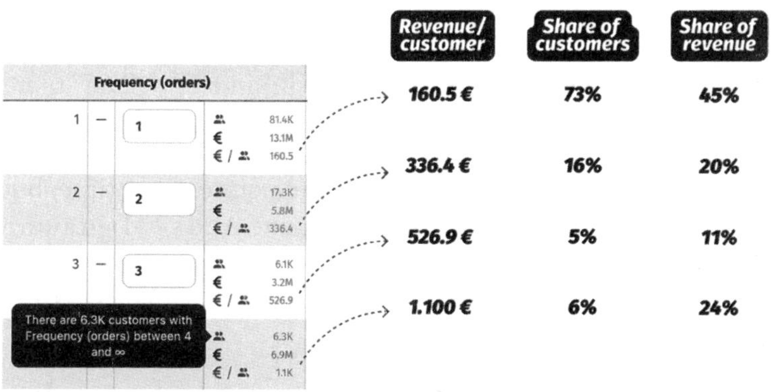

Returning to our example company, if you want to address the top 6 percent of your customers, those who generate

24 percent of your revenue, you have to use a scale from **1 to 4**. However, if you're using a scale of **1 to 3**, then you wind up blending in these "super consumers" with your "good, not great" customers.

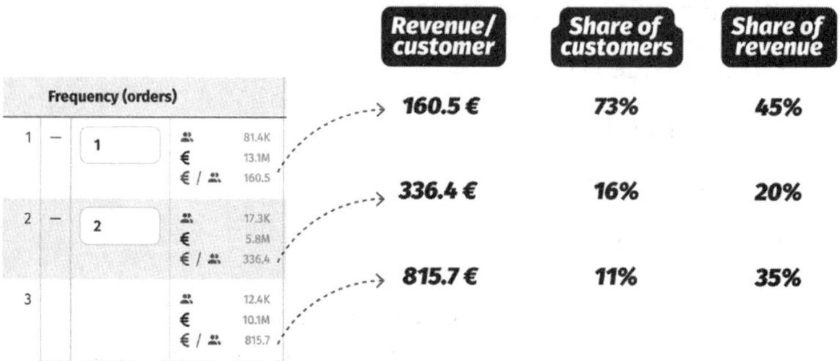

Doing so would cause you to miss some extremely valuable insight, especially when you consider that customers in your **4+ group** are twice as valuable (monetarily speaking) when you compare them to your **3 group**.

Great, but what can you do with 64 clusters of customers? There are too many to handle, right? Well, you must have patience because, eventually, we will indeed blend them together. First, let's turn our focus toward Recency points.

I have been wrestling with this idea for quite some time, but I finally had the proverbial "a-ha!" moment. And yes, I am aware that some dogmatic traditional marketers might challenge the following, but here is how I applied the notion of a scoring scale to measure Recency

First, with a scale of **1 to 4**, using percentiles to set up your Recency points is misleading. That's because when you set up the Recency points, they will be heavily dependent on the seasonality. Here is a visual illustration:

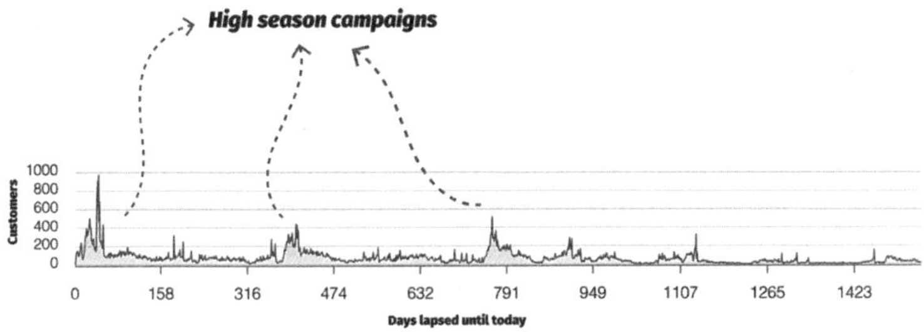

If you were to be setting up Recency points today, you would be relying on skewed data. That's why I use the average days between transactions or ADBT. Doing so looks like this:

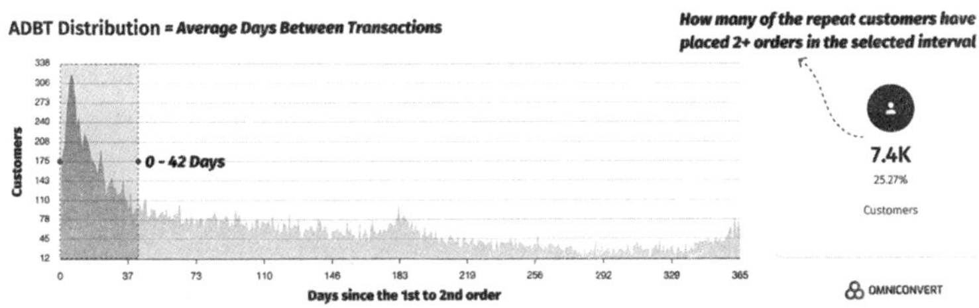

In the end, we are not really interested in how long it has been since a customer purchased. Instead, we want to determine how likely it is that the customer is still "alive" (active), plus the percentage of customers out there who are contemplating future purchases. This is another reason I suggest using percentiles from the ADBT distribution to set the Recency points.

Creating Customer RFM Segments

Once you have set the RFM scores, you are ready to create segments. Below I have provided a breakdown of how it works, along with some suggested names for your segments that I refer to throughout the rest of the book, especially when in part 3's conversation about campaigns. To understand at a practical level how RFM analysis should be made, I will share a file along with homework at the end of this chapter.

To begin, a customer can have a single score for R, F, and M at any given moment. If you are using a scale from **1 to 4**, I don't suggest using more than sixty potential segments. Below I have created a much simpler and smaller breakdown using ten RFM segments. Keep in mind that any RFM segment should contain at least two thousand customers in order to be able to run email or ad campaigns. However, if you sell very expensive products and you can use other expensive channels, you can form groups with fewer customers.

Soulmates

Soulmates are the absolute cream of the crop, the upper percent of the upper percent. This segment is particularly useful for larger companies with more than a million customers as a way to separate the highest scoring customers from a larger Lovers segment (which follows). Scoring for Soulmates looks like this:

- R = 4
- F = 4
- M = 4

Lovers

Just below Soulmates, Lovers are also ideal customers. Their scoring looks like this:

- R = 4
- F = 3-4
- M = 4

Soulmates and Lovers have so much affinity for your products, services, and your company, it is as if they are out there in the world working on your behalf. They find enough value in your products, as well as the customer experience.

- They will come back to buy from you again and again, despite any obstacles.
- They will also happily hype your brand and tell their friends to buy your products, read your blog, subscribe to your newsletter, follow your social media channels, etc.
- These customers are extremely profitable. You paid the cost to acquire them once, and they've built the habit of buying from you again and again.

In fact, these customers have such an affinity for your company they create an almost disproportionate amount of value. You don't have to do much to keep them happy. You've won their love (almost) forever.

Apprentices

These are newly acquired customers with low to average Monetary scores. Their scoring looks like this:

- R = 4
- F = 1
- M= 1, 2, 3

New Passions

These are also newly acquired customers, but they have the highest Monetary scores. Here is a look at their scoring:

- R = 4
- F = 1
- M = 4

Potential Lovers

These are active, but somewhat mediocre customers when it comes to Frequency and Monetary spend. Their scoring breaks down as follows:

- R = 3-4
- F = 2-3
- M = 1-3

Not to Lose

These customers used to be Lovers or New Passions but are slipping away. Their Recency and Monetary spend remain high, but their Frequency has dipped:

- R=3
- F =1-4
- M = 4

About to Dump You

Much like your Not to Lose customers, those in the About to Dump You group are also slipping away. The difference is that their Recency and Monetary spend have been average from the get-go:

- R = 2
- F = 1-4
- M = 1-3

Ex-Lovers

As the name suggests, these customers used to be Lovers, but now they have churned through the Not to Lose category and are on the streets looking for someone new. Can you win them back?

- R =1
- F = 3-4
- M = 4

Don Juans

This is an interesting group of "one-time only" customers. They placed a single order a long time ago but no longer hold up as New Passions since they never came back. Still, their memory runs hot:

- R= 1
- F = 1
- M =4

Breakups

These are low-value customers that have come and gone:

- R = 1
- F =1-4
- M = 1-3

Moving Between RFM Segments

Customers transition from segment to segment all of the time. Here's a visual I made using the skills I gained during the "bad old days," when I needed to find new ways to support my family as a designer after a few bad entrepreneurial bets:

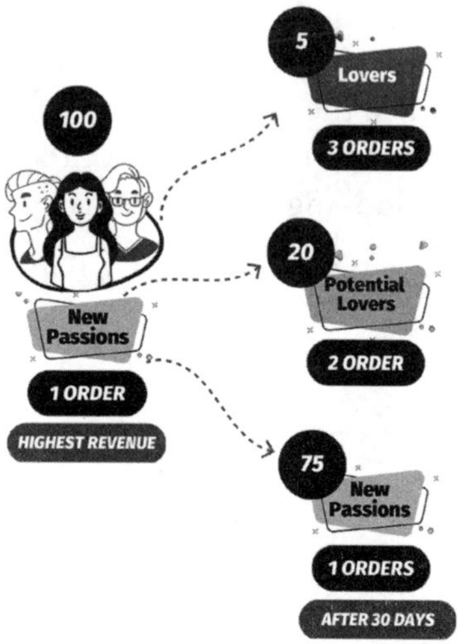

All joking aside, this visual is actually useful as we consider how customers move around. Let's look at New Passions, for instance, starting with what happens 30 days after their first purchase:

- 5 percent place two more orders and become Lovers.
- 20 percent place one order and become Potential Lovers.
- 75 percent do not place another order and remain New Passions.

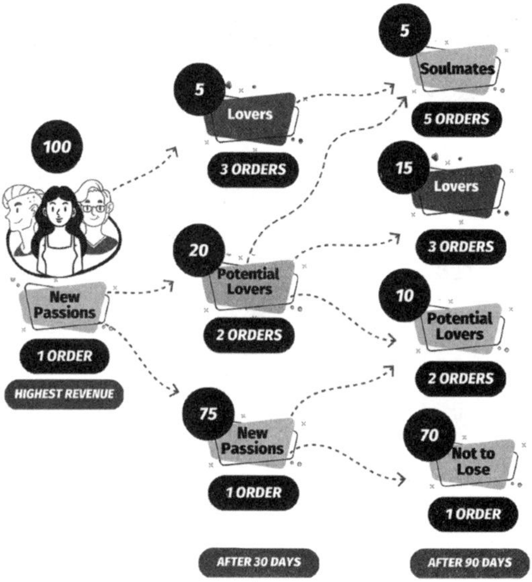

Now let's look at what happens 90 days after their first purchase:

- 70 percent do not place another order. They move from New Passions to Not to Lose (since their first order had a high Monetary spend).
- 10 percent remain in the Potential Lovers segment
- 15 percent are still Lovers
- 5 percent have jumped from Lovers to the Soulmate segment, as their R, F, and M scores are off the charts.

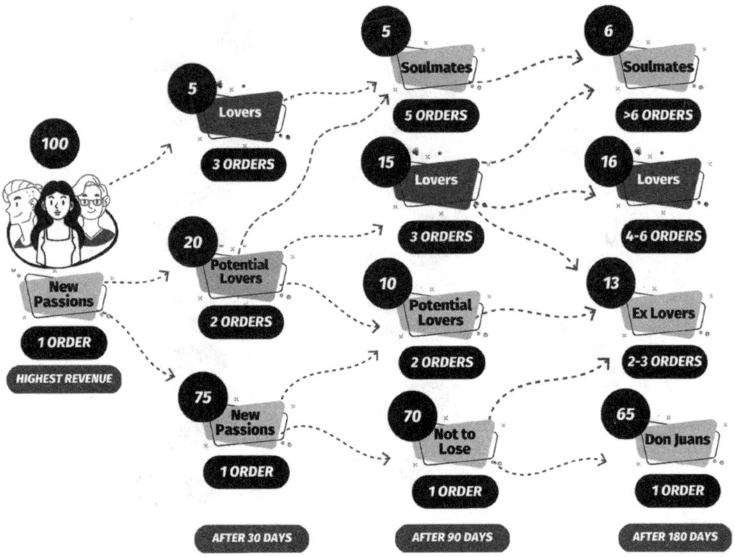

Finally, let's explore what happens 180 days after their first purchase:

- 65 percent of the New Passions still haven't placed another order and have slipped into the Don Juan segment.
- 13 percent of them are now Ex-Lovers. They have placed four or more orders, but their Recency has dropped off.
- A combined 22 percent of these customers exist between your Lovers and Soulmates segments.

Considering the Cost of Customer Acquisition

Here is a tricky part of all of this: How much did it cost you to acquire different customers to begin with? You probably can't go back in time and recreate the moment when someone first discovered your brand, but it isn't impossible to track your acquisition costs. How then? Well, you can ask them as part of the customer research work I'll discuss in chapters 5 and 6. I'll put a pin in the deeper parts of this thought, but I did want to bring it into the conversation. The main point to understand for now is the following:

- Who are your super consumers (Soulmates and Lovers)?
- Why do they buy?
- How do they buy?

When you boil everything down, you discover quite a few differences between customer types. To unpack these differences and go beyond the revenue they generate, one natural step is to subtract the costs you spent to acquire them in the first place.

Let's say that the average order value (AOV) of a customer is $100, but it costs you $20 to acquire that same customer. In addition, let's say your margin is 40 percent. When you subtract the $20 you spent to acquire them, you only keep $20 from this customer's one-time purchase.

If you've built your business model on an ongoing stack of one-time customers, you're constructing a house of cards. The churn and burn will catch up to you, and your stack will go up in flames.

What happens when you focus on creating repeat customers? Use the same AOV ($100) acquisition costs ($20) and the 40 percent margin. This time, instead of customers being one-time shoppers, let's suppose they land in your "Lover" segment and place ten, one-hundred-dollar orders. When you subtract the $20 you spent to acquire them, this customer generates $380 in profit. That's 19X more than your one-time customers generate.

Again, this is a very simplified example, but the point is to offer another glimpse into how important it is to extend a customer's lifetime.

Using Information Customers Give You

The business climate as we know it is all about individuation and relevance. Not everyone is interested in "the best price" or "the most creative opportunity." They want products and services that are relevant to them and their respective journeys. Knowing who your best customers are, requires getting out of the trap that e-commerce "gurus" and big media companies continue to sell—that all you need to grow is to buy ads.

This brings me to another story from back when I was selling car insurance, one of those serendipitous and important stops along my professional journey.

Car insurance means something very different to motorists, depending on what, where, and how they drive. Our company was struggling and didn't grasp this notion. We saw car insurance as an annual commodity and were in a constant state of acquisition. We also did not pay attention to Recency and Frequency, and focused mainly on Monetary spend.

I spent most of my time diving into Google analytics, obsessed with the data. I could not find anything to resolve our churn and burn situation. Then I realized that I was looking at the wrong thing. I instructed our team to start gathering data that explored the makes and models of cars our customers drove. Was there something useful hiding in this qualifying piece of data? What were they buying coverage for?

Per the data, our best customers either drove trucks, or owned luxury cars. In both cases, their insurance premiums were higher than average car owners. Using this information, I explored their AOV, and discovered that these drivers generated nearly 60 percent of our total margin, even though they made up only 15 percent of our customer base.

This was a eureka moment for us. From then on, we shifted our marketing dollars, sales, and the focus of our customer service toward these customer segments. We also doubled down on how we approached CLV.

This anecdote points to a key business truth: Gathering data is only one more piece of the equation. However, if you are not going to do anything with the data, then you are simply wasting more time. Again, we could have continued to throw money at blindly pursuing acquisitions without taking a more targeted approach. But updating the copy with empty campaign language does not move the needle. You can try to improve your Google search, SEO, or organic and paid content, but the results will not change until you focus on what your ideal customers are trying to tell you.

Building Your Ideal Customer Profile (ICP)

Your ideal customers (Soulmates and Lovers) hold the key. They are the people who shop with you. It's time to discover their motivations and pivot your actions in this direction. That's how you will find more customers like them.

If you are struggling to make it, you can't afford to do what everyone else is doing. You need to take some moon shots. There are customers that you simply cannot miss. They're the ones that make you a lot of money.

It's about focus. If you run after too many rabbits, you'll catch none. That is why you need to begin to develop your Ideal Customer Profile (ICP)

**when you compare their Customer Lifetime Value*

My eyes popped the first time I made this calculation. If you compare the CLV of a Soulmate or a Lover with the CLV of an Apprentice, for instance, their values are dramatically different. You will have to see for yourself with your own numbers. When you do, you will never unsee it. That's why developing the ICP is a key part of the work that comes out of building your RFM segmentation. It gives you a bullseye, so you can identify the customers that you simply cannot miss in your marketing efforts.

At the end of the day, it would be wonderful and much easier if you could simply rely on a big net effect: toss the biggest, broadest, most general message out into the world and let it pull as many fish back as possible. But if you've been in the e-commerce game for a while now, then you know this is an unsustainable model.

Your customers have reasons why they choose you to begin with; they also have reasons why they stay. Sometimes, these reasons are not the same. When you include acquisition costs in your thinking, you begin to see that the more powerful net effect comes from those customers who return and return again. Taking their needs into account, and building your ICP around them, helps you build a more targeted spend around your next round of acquisition.

Continue to Make Space for All Customers

Let me be clear about what it means to put your ICP to work for you. These efforts are about more than focusing and marketing to your best customers, but about prioritizing the ones who matter.

As you build programs around these customer types, you begin to shift your ads and marketing campaigns and craft messages around the things that matter to them. However, that does not mean that you suddenly turn the faucet off where other types of customers are concerned. You need them as well. Even though the margin may not be as good, you still need the revenue. I want to clarify this now so you avoid thinking that I am suggesting you niche your business and marketing efforts around the customer types that rise to the top of your ICP work. That's not the case.

The bigger idea is to prioritize your efforts around the needs of these customers in order to get more like them. In doing so, you do not want to refuse the others who come in. You have to figure out how to prioritize the right customer types and make sure you're not losing money on the other ones.

RFM segmentation is the first step toward categorizing your customers. From there, based on this work, your ideal customer (those in the "outstanding" label from earlier in this chapter), begins to rise to the top. From this information, you can begin to build your ICP.

It's time again to set the book down, and start your next round of homework.

Homework: RFM Segmentation

Go to our the following URL, and download our CVO Academy RFM Distribution Template:

RFM Group	All Customers	New Customers	Orders	Revenue	Margin	CRC (Customer Retention Cost)	CAC (Customer Acquisition Cost)	CLV (Customer Lifetime Value)	CLV/CAC	Parity vs the lowest-value first-time customers
Soulmate	1,373	430	12,977	$1,268,069	$561,211	$16		$1,289	71.6	204
Lover	7,004	4,123	34,556	$3,268,380	$1,461,930	$14		$341	18.9	54
New passion	3,543	2,687	5,853	$543,831	$225,795	$12		$72	4.0	11
Flirting	11,164	3,867	13,377	$1,685,069	$691,335	$8		$171	9.5	27
Potential lover	4,748	2,877	27,078	$1,698,941	$712,362	$8		$240	13.3	38
Platonic friend	25,973	9,846	37,890	$1,697,844	$717,327	$10	$18	$63	3.5	10
About to dump you	55,565	37,325	83,245	$5,084,904	$2,105,976	$4		$52	2.9	8
Don Juan	13,255	11,345	13,255	$2,034,199	$838,026	$3		$71	3.9	11
Ex lover	14,848	4,866	26,784	$2,009,327	$842,824	$12		$161	9.0	25
Apprentice	26,768	24,586	26,768	$688,052	$278,636	$5		$6	0.4	1
Breakup	15,896	12,547	16,878	$421,732	$168,925	$2		$11	0.6	2
All	**180,137**	**114,499**	**298,661**	**$20,400,346**	**$8,604,346**			**$87**	4.8	

BIT.LY/RFM-TEMPLATE

This user-friendly database format has gone through a number of iterations since I first built it a few years ago. Rather than build your own, this tool allows you to pull key data automatically.

After the download, I want you to get answers to these questions from your own dataset:

- What's the difference between your best customers and the lowest-value customers?
- What's the share of revenue generated last month by your best customer group? Is this moving on a positive or negative trend?
- How much of your marketing efforts are focused on first-time customers vs. on your existing customers?

And remember, your data means nothing if you don't take action on it.

Once you complete your RFM segmentation and begin to construct your ICP, the next steps unfold like this:

- Gaining a more in-depth understanding of what makes them buy.
- Building a retention strategy to keep them coming back and turning them into those outstanding brand advocates I discussed at the start of this chapter.
- Building an acquisition model that attracts others like them.

When you put RFM segmentation to work, you discover your best customers, understand why they buy, and begin pivoting your marketing toward attracting and retaining more people like them. Understanding your customer segmentation helps you begin to adapt to their needs and keep your products, services, and marketing relevant to them.

Once you know your customers, you'll be ready to find out what jobs they want to perform by hiring your products. We'll go in this direction in chapter five. In the meantime, enjoy your homework.

CHAPTER 5

Begin with the End in Mind

Chapter 4 covered a lot of ground, including creating your RFM segmentation and the importance of Ideal Customer Profiles (ICP). Let's move forward in our understanding and take a deeper dive into conducting qualitative research and getting to know more about your top customers.

You Can't Just Skim the Surface

To know your customers, you must go deep to discover what motivates them to buy your products, support your brand, and tell others about you. When you understand how they see your brand, you can see how they define the "jobs," meaning the benefits your products perform.

When you know the job, you can work backward to find ways to connect customer motivations with the intended results. With this in mind, I want to explore how Clayton Christensen and Bob Moesta's "Jobs to Be Done" (JBTD) methodology applies to e-commerce businesses.

A note before I go forward: JTBD is a part of the CVO methodology, but it is mainly impactful for direct-to-consumer companies that don't have hundreds or thousands of SKUs. If you are a retailer that sells products from different brands, JTBD can still be useful, but the focus will be on uncovering why customers create the habit of buying from your store, not why they buy the products you sell.

Customers Buy Results, Not Products

The JTBD framework makes clear that people don't want to just own products or use services. Instead, they want to make progress in their lives with the help of your products. Using the JTBD framework helps you see the jobs that your products perform through the eyes of your best customers. With this knowledge, you can begin to emphasize these benefits in an effort to attract more soulmate customers.

If you're unfamiliar with Clayten Christensen's work, there's a lot of information online about the JTBD framework and how he developed it from theory to concept. It goes beyond marketing research and uncovers the deeper "why" behind any purchase, which points to the "job" that a customer wants a product to perform. His book *The Innovator's Solution,* published in 2003, presents the story of JTBD in great detail. A few years ago, the JTBD framework was something we walked into, not as a way to study it, but as a way to turn our business around.

We wanted to understand our ICP and ended up getting help from Bob Moesta as we interviewed our customers about the "why" that led to their purchases. This eventually led to us turning our ship from Conversion Rate Optimization to Customer Value Optimization, where we still focus today.

When a Blanket is More Than a Blanket

Weighted blankets have been around for a few years. They started to go mainstream in 2017 when companies drew a link between the blankets and modern sleep science. Prior to this, a weighted blanket brand hired us to help improve their SEO and generate sales. At the time, their marketing touted various touch and texture benefits, along with seasonal promises: how soft, warm, comfortable, and cozy the blankets were, for instance. These types of characteristics were accurate, but their messaging wasn't moving the needle to help sales. Still, they had built something of a cult following among customers who kept coming back to buy more. However, the data they gathered was disparate at best. They couldn't quite explain why some people kept coming back, whereas others were one-and-done buyers.

They were one of our first clients to go all-in on using RFM segmentation methodology. In fact, convincing them to implement the RFM strategy was not a challenge. However, they were still highly assumptive of what their products were all about—again, a weighted blanket is a weighted blanket, right?

Let me reiterate something I've shared already: Bias is a common problem for many business owners, even ones who are excited by change, and are open to something new. In this case, the company was biased by its assumptions of what its product was all about. They judged their product based on its physical reality (a soft, warm, cozy weighted blanket). And they built their campaigns and SEO strategy around the same things, highlighting comfort and coziness. Yet their campaigns weren't moving the sales needle. They were looking at the product but not at its job. To understand the job that their soulmate customers had in mind, we needed to go to the source and speak with the customers themselves.

Discovering Jobs To Be Done with Weighted Blankets

After completing the RFM segmentation, similar to your own work at the end of chapter 4, we selected a group of about a dozen customers who fell into the Soulmate category (those with the highest RFM score). Many of these customers had bought blankets for themselves, then came back to buy a second as a household spare, then came back again to buy the blankets for friends and family.

As we dove into deeper interviews, our goal was to understand how they defined the blanket's job. Were they buying the blankets because they were warm and cozy? Not exactly. Here are a few of the reasons why they bought blankets again and again:

- In almost every case, the blankets helped to solve sleep problems.
- Some people used the blankets when they were feeling sad, alone, or even depressed.
- The blankets also helped them cope when they were dealing with illness or other medical conditions.

I've highlighted these three as a way to illustrate how quickly different threads begin to appear when you are conducting JTBD interviews. Perhaps we could have stopped here, but as I said at the start of the chapter, you can't skim the surface. These answers took us down a layer, but we needed to go deeper. Specifically, we wanted to explore the link between how the blankets helped to improve issues related to the quality of life.

One interviewee, in particular, stands out. She told us that she had been desperate for sleep but could not use sleeping pills. Her husband was quite ill, and she was his primary caretaker. She could not afford to fall so deeply asleep that she couldn't wake up if he needed her in the middle of the night. For her, the weighted blanket was actually a miracle cure. When she used it, she slept better than she had ever slept, and yet she could wake up to the sound of his voice calling her.

We began to hear similar details as we talked to other people. To these soulmate customers, the weighted blanket was much more than a cozy luxury item to keep around the house. They had become must-have parts of their overall health. Working from this perspective, we landed on the premise that the most important job the blankets performed boiled down to helping people lead healthier lives thanks to better sleep without taking sleeping pills.

Building Campaign Initiatives with the Help of JTBD

As with everything in the CVO methodology, the JTBD work is not an end-all-be-all situation. It points the way forward and helps you see where to go next. Here, I'd like to share how what we uncovered during our JTBD research helped our weighted blanket client pivot their own strategy.

- Following the deep-dive JTBD interviews, we constructed an online and email survey to capture insights from more customers across the RFM spectrum. Among the questions, we asked them to rate their sleep before and after they began using their weighted blankets.
- We also asked people if they had been dealing with any medical concerns or conditions prior to using the blankets. This was a Yes/No question with an optional comments field. Many people shared that they had suffered from insomnia and anxiety and that the blankets helped them to achieve better sleep despite symptoms.
- Finally, in these surveys, people shared different ways that the blanket had helped improve their quality of life. It wasn't only about sleep. Many people shared that the blanket's cuddling effect helped them overcome feelings of sadness or isolation.

These insights led to an interesting conclusion: The jobs of our client's product aligned with health choices. For customers, these blankets were not just nice-to-haves but must-haves. This was a critical *aha* for us and our client.

People Do Not Buy Products

Conducting Jobs to Be Done research can be eye-opening for any company. Since working with the weighted blanket client, we have led more than a dozen companies through the Jobs to Be Done methodology in order to understand what their soulmate customers thought of their products and solutions.

The results point to the same conclusion: Whether you sell blankets, oils, furniture, energy drinks, or something else, your customers are not buying your product. They are buying the results that the product produces and the change it brings to their lives. They are struggling with something in their lives, and your product helps them reduce or eliminate the struggle. That is the job fulfilled with your product's help.

Working from this mindset, you can begin to think of your products as vehicles that take consumers from point A to point B and get answers to questions such as the following:

- In what ways do your products transport people?
- What are their desired outcomes?
- What context made them say today is the day I am buying this product?
- What alternatives do they have, rather than using your product?
- How does your product change their lives for the better?

When you know these answers, you can redirect and refocus your messaging to highlight this transfer from one state of being to another. Otherwise, you will continue to shoot in the dark with messages that focus on the assumed feature sets of the products: the cozy comfort of a blanket, for instance, but not the fact that the weighted blanket was the best natural way to sleep better without being knocked out by the sleeping pills.

The beauty of conducting JTBD research involves finding out the reasons why people buy your products and also coming to understand what kind of progress they want to make in their lives. When you know the progress they want to make, you also know the struggles they want to move away from. This insight makes your job as a marketer much easier and more impactful:

- When you hear, for instance, that your product helps people attain better sleep, this can become a targeted message right away. It opens doors to stronger, value-added acquisition propositions.
- Following these threads can bring more soulmates and recurring shoppers your way. That's because the benefit speaks to them, and they want to extend this benefit to others who share the same struggle.

Putting the JTBD methodology to work for you is a reminder that you are not selling products but are selling solutions to problems. In the end, the problem is the thing that has energy and can be a catalyst that drives purchasing decisions.

Optimize Your Product Assortment

Wait, I wrote that "people don't buy products" only a few paragraphs ago, and now I'm telling you to "optimize your product assortment." I must be crazy. Actually, this is a critical message that will pair with the insights you'll gain when you start to put NPS to work for you (more on this in chapter 6).

I'm going to end this chapter by getting you ready to put JTBD to work. Before I get there, I want to make sure you are thinking about your products in terms of the jobs they do, so you can build a solid picture of whether or not your products are fulfilling their jobs, and making people happy. You have to look at the metrics to find which are your best and worst products.

The CVO Methodology

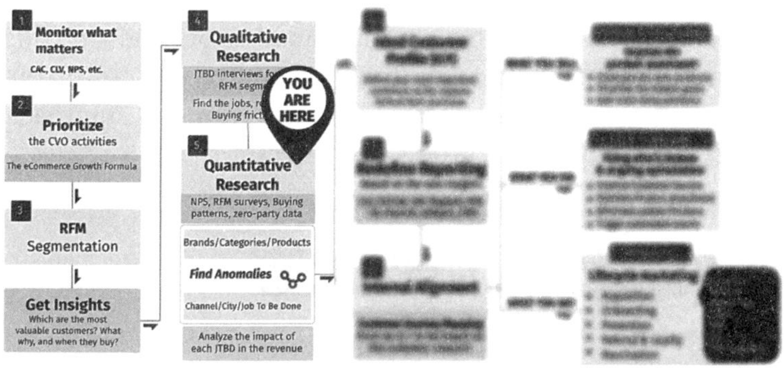

Even though product optimization is one of the most impactful pillars of the CVO game, it remains neglected, in part for two reasons:

1. Chaotic reporting. Without customer-centric reporting that comes from the top of the company, each department's leader sets narrow KPIs. Even when they improve things in the silo, they might actually harm the organization. What if marketing wants to sell product X, merchandising wants to move product Y, and the CFO just wants more profit? Where's the customer in this shell game?

2. Disconnected silos. Lack of internal alignment comes with chaotic reporting. Marketing has some KPIs, but merchandising has others. So does customer support, for that matter. This fractured approach harms the company and erodes CLV.

There are three decisions you can make in order to reach a more integrated product optimization perspective:

1. Get rid of toxic products.
2. Prioritize sticky products.
3. Add new sticky products to your offer.

For retailers that don't have a large number of products, this optimization endeavor is pretty simple once you finish the layers of qualitative research. To start, you can approach things by looking at the product return rate:

Now take a look at the graphic below. These figures can help you understand if you have toxic products:

Buying trends by purchased product

for customers who had a specific Product in First purchase in the following time interval 2022-01-15 - 2023-01-15

Show variants

	Product	Customers	Orders	Revenue	Margin	CLV	AOV	Chance to place 2nd order	Product Return rate
596	Gorgeous Plastic Pants	352.00	639.00	386.6K	145.5K	489.34	604.93	4.46%	12.70%
49185	Incredible Cotton Car	339.00	697.00	373.9K	129.6K	643.18	536.50	6.70%	8.26%
31910	Small Cotton Hat	330.00	708.00	427.2K	159.5K	779.63	603.42	5.48%	8.98%
571	Gorgeous Concrete Car	298.00	561.00	308.5K	110.9K	684.14	549.96	4.86%	9.06%
64	Incredible Plastic Table	298.00	661.00	425.5K	160.7K	841.01	643.71	4.34%	10.23%
47972	Small Concrete Gloves	287.00	735.00	392.6K	136.9K	849.34	534.09	7.63%	6.69%
53355	Gorgeous Plastic Car	267.00	490.00	239.3K	79.2K	559.41	488.45	6.35%	7.02%
39410	Gorgeous Plastic Shirt	239.00	470.00	249.0K	86.0K	632.88	529.73	6.01%	10.59%

OMNICONVERT

- Look at the "Gorgeous Plastic Pants" line item, for instance. Even though it generates high revenue and has a very good CLV, it also has the highest product return rate (12.7 percent).
- On the other hand, if you look at "Small Concrete Gloves," it has the highest CLV, the highest chance to place a second order, and the lowest product return rate, Translation: customers that buy this product are happier than all other customers.
- Finally, the "Incredible Plastic Table" generates the highest CLV, but also has the lowest chance of making the customers come back and a high return rate.

Show the customers metrics in 2022-02-08 - 2023-02

for customers who had a specific Product in First purchase in the following time interval 2022-02-08 - 2023-02

Show variants

Look at these 2 products. Almost the same AOV, almost the same Revenue, but dramatically different CLVs

Apply

Eid	Name	Customers	CLV	Orders	Revenue	Margin	AOV	Chance to place 2nd order
product-24936	Fujifilm Instax Mini	765.00	78.70	877.00	378.2K	[illegible]0.3K	431.26	11.11%
product-76237	DJI Mini 2 Fly More Combo	603.00	401.58	770.00	2.6M	135.9K	3.4K	18.91%
product-[illegible]	Godox LED 308IIC Lampa LED Bi-color 21W 3300-[illegible]	538.00	340.98	720.00	359.6K	107.9K	499.45	26.21%

Take a look at the example above from a retailer that sells digital cameras and accessories. If you look at the differences between these two products, you can see that the CLV is more than four times higher for customers that start their buying journey with Godox than with Fujifilm. With this data at hand, the retailer knows they can invest more toward acquiring Godox buyers and prioritize those products differently, as the untapped potential for those customers is considerably higher.

Whatever path you take to look deeper into your products, use a proven process. My team and I have connected many of these dots and built a product optimization framework to help open-minded retailers, agencies, and consultants make this type of shift.

The 4 Data Layers Product Optimization Framework

This process works for midsize and large retailers that have many SKUs and want to prioritize what matters. I realized the need for this framework while working closely with a shoe retailer that had just introduced a new brand. The demand and sales were high for the product, but the retention and CX data were very low. Here is a glimpse at how the framework operates:

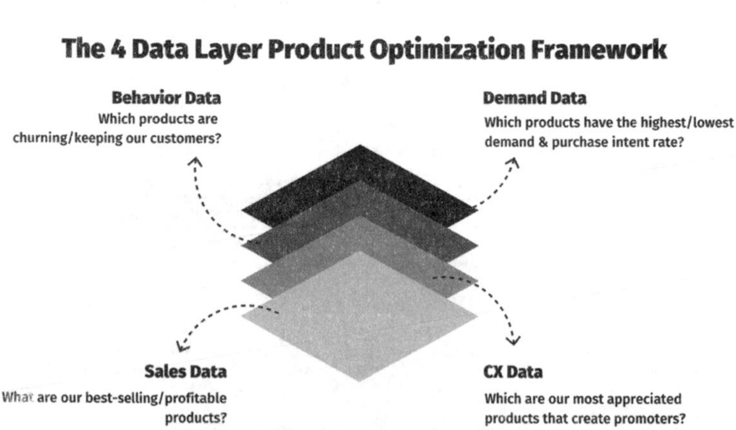

1. The Sales Volume Layer

This is the most common type of data. It's easy to extract from tools like Google Analytics or your e-commerce OMS. For our purpose (to identify the best products and get rid of toxic products), this isn't the best help, however, as it only answers questions about the past, not the future. For instance, you will be able to answer things like:

- Which are our best-selling products?
- Which are the most profitable products?

However, to rate and compare products based on the sales data, you must blend things like revenue, margin, and number of orders together. Doing so will give you an aggregate sales score. For example:

	Share of Revenue (40% weight)	Share of Margin (60% weight)	Sales Score
Product 1	28%	22%	**58.2%**
Product 2	34%	46%	**95.8%**
Product 3	38%	32%	**81.7%**

2. The Customer Experience Layer

To pull this data, you need answers to two crucial questions:

1. Which are the most appreciated products? You can get this answer from product reviews, whether you are capturing them by brand, product, or category. You can pull data from reviews using any number of review apps, such as Trustpilot, Reviews.io, or Yotpo, to name

a few. If you don't have enough reviews on your shop, you can find reviews about the products that you're selling on other websites (Amazon.com, for instance). This can also be a good method to identify relevant SKUs if you're looking to expand your catalog with products that are sticky enough.

2. How appreciated are your products? This answer involves getting the NPS by product, brand, and category. Again, there's much more coming about NPS in chapter 6, including how to pull these numbers. I want to share this piece now as you think deeper about adding new data layers as ways to identify products that people love.

	NPS (50% weight)	Review Score (50% weight)	CX Score (normalized)
Product 1	67%	4.54	85%
Product 2	81%	4.56	92%
Product 3	91%	4.76	100%

3. The Behavior Data Layer

This perspective takes into account what happens post-purchase with the customers that bought those products. It answers questions like the following:

- Which products are affecting positively or ruining our relations with our customers?
- Which are the products that are bought by our most loyal customers?

In order to get this data, you can use the categories I've shared already:

- CLV by-product
- Chance to place the second order
- Purchase frequency (PF)
- Product return rate

To rate and compare various attributes, you can normalize them:

	CLV	PF	Chance for the 2nd Order	Product Return Rate
Product 1	$78.00	3.20	16.5%	11%
Product 2	$91.00	2.10	22.5%	9.50%
Product 3	$102.00	2.89	18.9%	11.45%

	CLV Score (normalized)	PF Score (normalized)	Chance for the 2nd Order Score (normalized)	Product Return Rate Score (normalized)	Behavior Score
Product 1	76%	100%	73%	96%	86%
Product 2	89%	66%	100%	83%	84%
Product 3	100%	90%	84%	100%	94%

Notice I included the product return rate as a standalone metric. That's because two products with the same CLV can have very different return rates. That means one is more profitable than the other.

4. **The Demand Data Layer**

If you sell products that customers love but demand remains low, what can you do? This is an important question to answer and a reminder that you must always keep an eye on how attractive your products are in the market. To gather this data, you have to look at whatever web analytics tool you use. Most marketers also look for conversion rates by traffic source, location, or device.

An important aspect here is to identify and monitor the conversion rate by product. After all, you are investing a ton of money in ads and building web traffic for various products. You want them to convert into sales, right?

What if you could monitor the conversion rate at the product level so that you can see which products convert the best and which cost you the least to sell?

To maximize the demand data layer, you have to blend together buy-to-detail-rate, product-view rate, cost-per-conversion, and traffic volume:

	Buy-to-detail-rate (normalized)	Product View Rate (normalized)	Share of views (normalized)	CPO (normalized)	Demand Score
Product 1	97%	100%	90%	96%	**96%**
Product 2	57%	97%	60%	83%	**74%**
Product 3	100%	60%	100%	100%	**90%**

In the end, it's up to you to decide how to weigh these four data parameters and calculate an opportunity score that will guide your marketing decisions as you go forward.

	Sales Score (30% weight)	CX Score (10%)	Behavior Score (40%)	Demand Score (20%)	Opportunity Score
Product 1	58%	85%	86%	96%	**80%**
Product 2	96%	64%	84%	74%	**84%**
Product 3	82%	69%	94%	90%	**87%**

This work can be truly transformative for your company and guide you toward a comprehensive merchandising strategy. You'll discover all sorts of products, from hidden gems to simple stones, as you can see below:

Sales	Demand	CX & Behavior	Label	Action	Questions you want to answer
High	High	High	True gems	Keep on selling	*Are we giving those products the high priority they deserve?*
High	Low	Low	Fake diamonds	Investigate further	*Are those products not sticking due to low quality or over-expectations or is this due to their seasonality, low consumption pattern or longer purchase cycle?*
High	High	Low	Needs more polish	Investigate further	*Is the CX score so low and retention so high because of the poor quality and customers can't find proper product alternatives?Can we find other suppliers?*
High	Low	High	Shines, but not for long	Investigate further	*Is the retention low due to seasonality, lack of marketing efforts or purchase cycle?*
Low	High	High	Potential hidden gems	Prioritize them better	*Is the sales volume low due to lack of proper marketing efforts or due to low demand in the market?*
Low	Low	High	Rare, but loved	Investigate further	*Why are these products so recommended if the customers don't come back to buy again?*
Low	High	Low	Rare semi-precious	Investigate further	*Why is the retention so high, but CX so low?*
Low	Low	Low	Simple stones	Exclude from your merchandising efforts	*Are we giving those products the low priority they deserve?*

Understanding and applying this framework is a serious endeavor. You can find more information about the four data layers on the CVO academy website. Now, let's wrap up with a final look at putting JTBD to work for you.

Of course, we're working at Omniconvert to make this kind of analysis and product optimization completely automated.

Putting Jobs to Be Done to Work

To do JTBD research yourself, you have to focus on your best customers (those soulmates or lovers again), as they exhibit the type of customer behavior you want to replicate. You should also consider the products they buy throughout their customer journey and pick the ones that matter most for your business.

As you narrow your list of soulmate customers, try to get down to no more than twelve people to interview. The JTBD methodology suggests conducting interviews that last at least ninety minutes or as long as two hours. You're definitely at a moment where it will be helpful to have a team around you to support your efforts, whether from marketing, sales, customer service, or a mix of these focus areas.

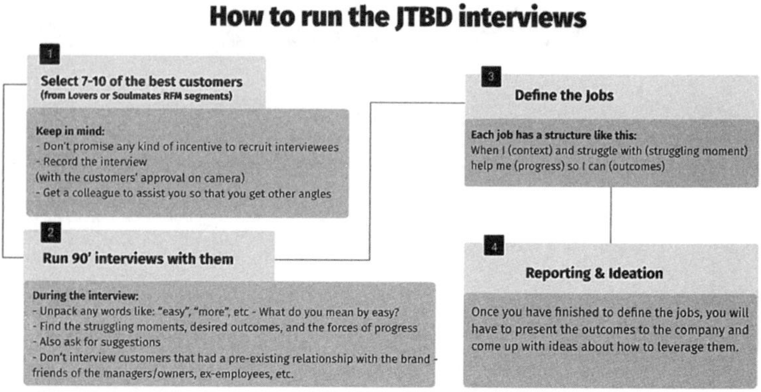

The JTBD framework is an ideal way to go deeper into why your best customers buy. The after-effects of putting the JTBD framework to use can be profound for your marketing and messaging. With these insights, you can improve the way you market, communicate and nurture more soulmate customers to make progress in their lives.

After gaining insights from the Jobs to Be Done methodology, you can begin to do the following:

- Update your web copy, email messaging, and targeted ads around keywords and key messages your soulmates share.
- Test different targeted ads across various media platforms.
- Craft a more relevant onboarding journey that helps your customers make progress - with or without your product.

Remember, everything people buy is attached to one struggle or another. When a person is buying something, it is the struggle that makes them search for solutions. They go from passive to active—from feeling the struggle to looking for something that will change their present state.

Eventually, they make a decision that helps them achieve progress in their life. And when they finally find the solution —and it's an especially great solution—they want to help other people who are dealing with the same struggle. Just like the buyers of weighted blankets who loved the product and recommended it to friends.

If you want to learn more about how to run a successful JTBD research, enroll in the free consumer behavior course on the CVO Academy - me and Bob Moesta will teach you how to run JTBD research and then leverage it in your company. This is especially impactful for DTC businesses.

BIT.LY/FREE-CVO-COURSE

Also, I highly recommend that you read Bob Moesta's book, *Demand Side Sales.*

What comes after JTBD research? More research! This time, quantitative research. This research will help you understand the financial impact of each of the jobs to get answers to these questions:

- What's the CLV of customers, depending on the jobs they hire your products for?
- What is the financial impact of each of the jobs?
- What is the distribution of the jobs for each of the RFM segments?

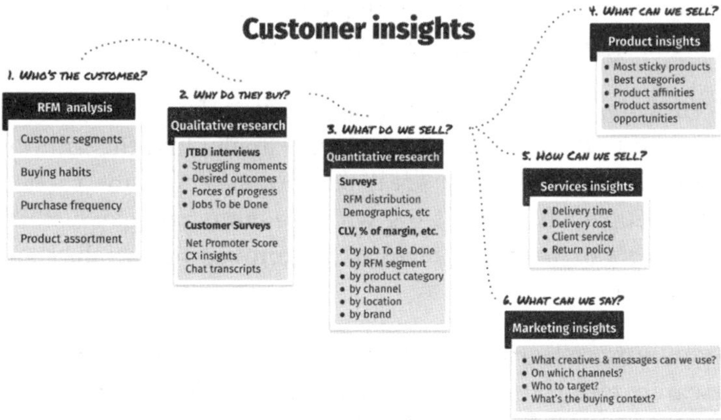

This process also involves getting to know your soulmates even better after you gain some in-depth insights from a handful of customer interviews. In time, you can continue to validate the importance of each job when it comes to recurring revenue and margin. To do so, you will run a larger but less in-depth round of surveys, using a greater span of customers. The process is pretty straightforward:

If you wonder what kind of insights you will need from each RFM segment, help is on the way in chapter 6. Before I take us there, let me remind you something that I can't stress enough: The reason you run customer research is to make it actionable. Insight without action is just an attractive distraction. You can tell yourself that you're doing important work, but really, you're just keeping busy.

Okay, enough of my soapbox. Let's go to chapter 6. You and I will start with Ideal Customer Profiles (ICPs), then focus on ways to become even more targeted in your messaging and execution.

CHAPTER 6

Who Buys What and Why?

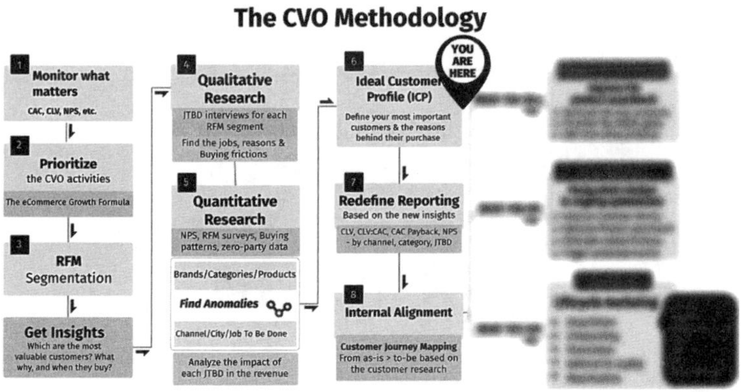

Here at the start of chapter 6, it's a good time to reiterate the 3 pillars of CLV growth:

- What you sell (Product)
- What you do (Customer experience)
- What you say (Marketing)

Obviously, there are various degrees of how solid those pillars are for each company. I suspect that something you've read thus far has made you reconsider these pillars in your own company. How would you rate how well your company is doing? Where are you strongest? Where do you need support? Hopefully, you feel confident enough to diagnose these pillars so as to know where you need to improve.

Not long ago, a direct-to-consumer customer of ours found themselves revisiting the three pillars. They were selling vegan keto nutritional supplements and dietary aids. We created their RFM segmentation to identify their best and worst customers and also ran customer surveys to find out the reasons behind an uptick in customer churn. What we discovered was that how the product tasted was creating low retention.

This was the worst scenario for them. As I wrote in chapter 3, marketing cannot fix a faulty product. Neither can a great customer experience. Just think about this for a moment. How can a company that sells consumable nutritional supplements retain customers when customers can't stand consuming their product? They can't! For that reason, pouring more money into the marketing machine was not an option for them. They had to optimize the product's taste before they could do anything.

I wanted to share this anecdote as a reminder of two things I have stressed already:

1. Gathering customer data is essential to your success.
2. Gathering data without acting on it is a colossal waste of time.

Matei, who runs our data wing at Omniconvert, once said to me after looking at a host of survey results: "All these weeks of work mining for product insights are nothing compared to what we've found by asking people these questions!"

	JTBD	NPS	DEMOGRAPHICS	REASONS LOST	REASONS WON	MAIN BARRIERS
SOULMATES	✓	✓	✓		✓	✓
LOVERS		✓	✓		✓	✓
APPRENTICE		✓	✓		✓	✓
NEW PASSIONS		✓	✓		✓	✓
POTENTIAL LOVERS		✓	✓		✓	✓
NOT TO LOSE		✓	✓	✓		✓
ABOUT TO DUMP YOU		✓	✓	✓		✓
EX-LOVERS		✓	✓	✓		✓
DON JUANS		✓	✓	✓		✓
BREAKUPS		✓	✓	✓		✓

Do You Sell X or Y?

Imagine that one night you go to bed thinking that you are selling slippers. In the morning, you discover that you really sell garden clogs. How did this happen? You can blame (or thank) your customers.

In chapter 5, you and I started to uncover some truths that came to the surface via Jobs to Be Done (JTBD) research and interviews. Let's go further with the help of Ideal Customer Profiles (ICPs), and the revenue that different jobs bring in.

Now that your JTBD interviews are in process (you're doing your homework, right?), let's find out what your best customers are thinking, how they're acting, and what their buying timelines, patterns, and decisions look like:

- What did they think when they chose you?
- What attracted them to your brand?
- How did they find you to begin with?
- What was their first purchase? Why?
- What keeps them coming back for more?

Context Creates Value, Contrast Creates Meaning

Let me ask the question again: Do you sell vitamins or painkillers? Some customers might think you sell painkillers. Others might think of your product as a vitamin. Within the CVO methodology, context creates value, while contrast creates meaning.

Your work, whether as a marketer or entrepreneur, is to put meaning to use. How? For starters, you want to make sure you're getting the most out of your JTBD interviews.

One of the most important parts of conducting JTBD interviews involves staying with a question for an extra beat or two. Since you are dealing with Soulmates, we can assume that they are happy about your company and your products. This is a good thing, but it can make things tricky when you are trying to go deeper with them.

For one, you don't want to push them away, especially if the conversations feel almost a little chatty. Plus, happy customers might tell you what they think you want to hear. They may be too willing to tout the things they love about you, especially in the first twenty or thirty minutes. That's why I suggest extending your interviews to 90 minutes or longer. This gives you more time to unpack nuances.

Hopefully, you'll be able to run these interviews and adjust your questions according to the free Consumer Behavior course from the CVO Academy - find the access to it in chapter 5.

Can it Taste Better?

My firm had a client that sold CBD oil. If you're unfamiliar, CBD refers to cannabidiol, a chemical from the cannabis plant. CBD oil does not include THC, the psychoactive compound in cannabis, and has been readily available for pain therapy since about 2015.

Our client was one of the first to attempt to break into the Australian market. They were convinced that they had the best product going. However, their customers had other thoughts, which we helped to uncover during JTBD research.

Again and again, people spoke openly about various jobs the product was performing in their lives. They were managing their pain, getting better sleep, enjoying happier moods, etc. And they liked the effects of the oil better than what they'd experienced with CBD pills. They also shared something the client wasn't expecting: They wished the product tasted better.

The word "better" is tricky. On its own, it doesn't give too much to work with. However, as a qualifier, it can lead you toward deeper, more specific questions. When we heard answers like, "I wish it tasted better," we asked for more information. Here's some more specific feedback we received:

- "By *better,* I really mean sweeter."
- "It leaves a bitter aftertaste."
- "I want to take it straight by the dropper, but I have to put it in tea to mask the flavor. I don't always want tea."
- "The greasy texture bothers me."
- "It almost made me gag the first few times I took it."

Do you remember the story from chapter 3 about the slick retailer that sold terrible products? When your product is broken, it's tough to turn the ship and move in a new direction. With our CBD clients, their Soulmates were saying that the product is great at its job or jobs, but the taste could use some help.

The company took this to heart. They revisited their formulation to address the taste and texture. They also took the issue and spun it into a series of campaign messages that focused on improved tastes and flavors. In other words, the JTBD feedback folded nicely into the campaign language.

Vitamin or Painkiller?

The Jobs to Be Done methodology also helps you prioritize your battles. Like it or not, not all jobs are equal. This is important to know as you take what your customers share and apply it.

How do you know which jobs are more important than others? How do you measure different jobs against each other? These answers can point the way forward when you roll out new campaigns or even redirect your business.

First, to know which jobs are more important, you have to analyze revenue. I'll stay in the area of alternative medicine and share the story of a client who sold turmeric shots. It was truly a fantastic product, even revolutionary in the minds of many of its customers. The company's founder is a former professional footballer, and during his career, turmeric shots helped him recover from injury. Leveraging his personal story, the company's marketing was geared toward younger athletes who wanted to recover faster and enjoy more energy on the playing field.

When we applied the Jobs to Be Done methodology and interviews, we uncovered a number of different messages as well as different jobs. A number of their Soulmate customers did fit their marketing strategy. They were young athletes, and the shots helped them recover after practices and games. When we cross-checked various jobs against revenue, an entirely different audience rose to the top: adults, middle-aged and older, who used the shots more like a daily vitamin. Here is some of what we heard:

- "I take one shot a day. It boosts my immune system! I can't afford to miss a day of work."

- "The shots help my arthritis more than anything else. I take one a day."
- "My doctor wants me to walk every day. I take a shot every morning, and now I'm up to almost five miles a day."

Suddenly, the job of the turmeric shots was different. People were taking the shots for pain relief, energy, and recovery, but they were doing it daily, not just after events. They played a more vital role in improving quality of life than our clients knew. And again, this insight came directly from their customers. This fact clearly showed in their revenue, especially when we looked into the Recency and Frequency of purchases.

The client was thrilled to gain this insight. It validated that their current marketing strategy, to connect with young athletes, was working. Bigger than that, it uncovered an entirely different customer base they didn't know they had. The skies were wide open for them to market in this previously unknown direction.

This insight also helped the client rethink their strategy around customer onboarding initiatives. I'll discuss onboarding campaign initiatives in much greater detail in chapter 10. For now, keep in mind that onboarding help builds a sense of continuity and connection between you and your customers. For example, if a majority of middle-aged customers use your product as a daily vitamin, but the majority of your onboarding messages focus on recovering after a big weekend football match, you risk missing a deeper connection. Our client was ready to improve their onboarding game, and create new Soulmates and Lovers.

Using Customer Data

In the last few chapters, we have narrowed down our RFM segmentation, explored the idea of products performing jobs, and cross-checked different jobs against revenue to rank them. This work is all about finding out what your best customers buy and why they keep buying it.

E-commerce customers are overwhelmed with choices. One way to help them stick with what they know is to remind them that you know them. How? By using customer data, of course. Let the insights from RFM and JTBD data guide you forward. To start, consider the following as you reflect on insights your customers give you:

- How many Soulmate do you have?
- What jobs do your products fulfill for Soulmates?
- Which jobs create the most revenue?
- How can you shift your marketing to highlight the best jobs?

Just imagine what could happen if you put more marketing money toward a high-performing job that you haven't even been marketing. And it all starts with your best customers and how well you get to know them.

The Role of Net Promoter Score

I love NPS! When you leverage it properly, it is like debugging the entire customer journey with the help of insights from hundreds or thousands of consumers. In an effort to improve CLV, even after you know your best customers, why they buy, and which jobs matter most, you need to continue to eliminate potential issues that can come up. How do you know what these issues are? Net Promoter Score is a great way to gather and compare feedback across various customer segments.

I find it amazing how many companies are not closing this feedback loop to check if their products actually "get the job done" for customers. They simply ignore what's known as the advanced e-commerce Growth Flywheel:

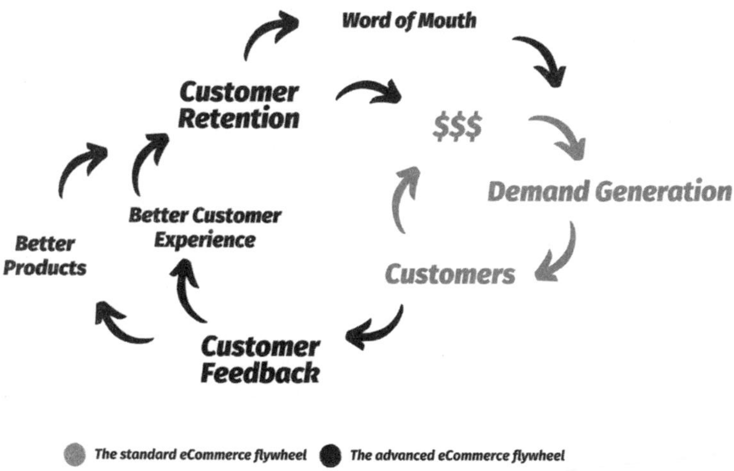

Creating and Using NPS Categories

You leverage the advanced Flywheel when you experiment, thanks to feedback you gain from actual customers. They're the ones that are actively testing out your products with every purchase. Not just the product but the entire experience—finding and choosing you, waiting, using the product, and reporting back via whatever actions follow.

How can you continue to pour money into acquiring new customers without knowing whether or not your product "did a good job"? NPS is a great way to close this loop. With the help of NPS, you can classify customers into three categories based on how they respond to this one single question:

> *On a scale of 0 to 10, how likely are you to recommend our products to a friend or colleague?*

Based on their answer, you will categorize each customer as being a Promoter, a Passive, or a Detractor.

Promoters

These customers give a score of 9 or 10. They are your most loyal group (soulmates and lovers again). It is highly likely that they will buy from you in the future and even recommend your company and products to friends, family, and coworkers.

Passives

These customers give a score of 7 or 8. They are satisfied with your products or services, but they may not be your most loyal or enthusiastic customers.

Detractors

These customers give you a score of 0 to 6. They are not satisfied with something and are unlikely to recommend you or your products to others. They may even switch to a competitor.

Calculating NPS

To calculate NPS, subtract the percentage of detractors from the percentage of promoters. This gives you your NPS, which will range from -100 to 100.

- A positive NPS indicates that you have more promoters than detractors. Well done!

- A negative NPS means that you have more detractors than promoters. Don't let this stress you out. Remember, the data offers a glimpse into what's happening. The actions you take on account of the data are what create change.

Staying with NPS

I ascribe to the belief that NPS should be a constant in every business. More ongoing customer research! This time, you'll measure NPS across all RFM segments. This can offer a snapshot of how customers across your entire consumer ecosystem perceive your company and rate their experiences.

Here's something else: This kind of diagnosis is helpful when you need to cure a past issue, but it's much better to prevent the issue from happening at all. That's why NPS is something you should monitor again and again and again.

Part of every customer's journey should involve sharing NPS at various moments. As a business, you give them a chance to do this with the help of the "thank you" message you send after purchase, via your email newsletter, at the bottom of their receipts, or even by calling them.

In the end, no matter where a customer lands on the 0-to-10 scale, their feedback is qualitative. They are sharing their subjective opinions. Eventually, you must turn these rankings into quantitative data, which I will get to shortly.

When to Send NPS Surveys

Here are the three important moments when you should monitor NPS:

1. **Pre-delivery**

   This happens when a customer is placing an order. You can include the NPS questionnaire right at the bottom of your "thank you" page. Tracking NPS pre-delivery helps you understand things like why they shopped in the first place, how they found you, and how easy they found the shopping experience to be.

2. **Post-delivery**

   This message goes out after a customer receives the product, often on the heels of a "your product has shipped!" message. Your post-delivery NPS message can cover ground like the 0-to-10 rating scenario I shared above. It can also focus exclusively on their experience with the product. For instance:

   - Does the product live up to your expectations?
   - Did it arrive in the condition you were expecting?

   Depending on what you learn from the customer research, you might also include a coupon in your post-delivery NPS message, or another targeted enticement to bring them back again.

3. **Post-usage**

   This message goes out a few days after they have received the product, or perhaps a week later. Some companies forgo the post-usage NPS message, depending on how comprehensive their post-delivery NPS message was.

   If you send post-deliver and post-usage NPS messages, the post-usage message is a good time to include something more extensive (assuming your post-delivery NPS message was on the lighter side). The timing of these messages heavily depends on the type of products. If your customers bought a slow-moving consumer item (a treadmill, a weighted blanket, etc.), then you'll want to trigger the post-usage NPS after enough time has passed to ensure that they've actually used the product for a little while.

Aiming for Delta NPS

One of the biggest benefits of collecting NPS throughout different moments in a customer's journey is to help you understand where you should be fixing things. Is there a significant difference between pre-delivery and post-usage or post-delivery NPS? What went wrong? Did the product not meet expectations? Conversely, do you notice an uptick in NPS after delivery? Did the product exceed expectations?

In the end, what you are aiming for is known as Delta NPS. When you are in the business of selling anything, you are actually in the business of selling a promise. The Delta NPS shows how well you fulfilled your promise.

This brings up an important question: Is there such a thing as a "great" or a "good" NPS? Here are some calculations for retailers:

- A great NPS is a score of 80 or above. This shows that your company has a very high level of customer satisfaction and loyalty.
- A good NPS is a score between 50-80. This shows that the majority of customers are likely to recommend the company to others.
- A mediocre NPS is lower than 50. This means your company has a balanced mix of promoters, passives, and detractors.

NPS and CLV

How does Net Promoter Score affect Customer Lifetime Value? I've seen data that suggests a Promoter's lifetime value can be 14X higher than a Detractor's. Here are some examples from clients:

- A mid-sized retail client of ours recently faced some turbulence. They grew too much and could not scale their team fast enough to keep up. At the same time, their NPS dropped from 78 to 71, while their CLV dropped from $142 to $119. The correlation shows that a 9 percent drop in NPS corresponded with a 17 percent drop in CLV.
- A mid-sized office supply store grew its NPS from 81 to 92 in two years, a jump of 12 percent. At the same time, their CLV grew 44 percent. This company also happens to be extremely customer-centric. They use real-time NPS alerts based on a strategy that I will discuss shortly. Their customer success team gets alerts whenever Soulmates or Lovers give low NPS scores. When an alert goes off, these customers receive immediate attention.

In both cases, data led to insight, but taking action was where the real work happened. If you want to build a terrible NPS strategy, here's what to do: Gather data, discover the insight, then ignore it completely. Or, if you want to build a strong and meaningful NPS strategy, step into action and put NPS to work across all RFM segments.

Mind the Average Trap

Whenever you look at average figures, it's easy to be misguided. If you have traveled or lived in the USA, then I assure you that the weather in St. Louis is much different than the weather in San Francisco. However, they technically have the same "average temperature." What gives?

You have to slice data down to the nubs to understand what's really happening. That goes for the weather but also CLV, revenue, and our friend NPS. You have to take into account how NPS varies based on many different angles. Consider the following diagram:

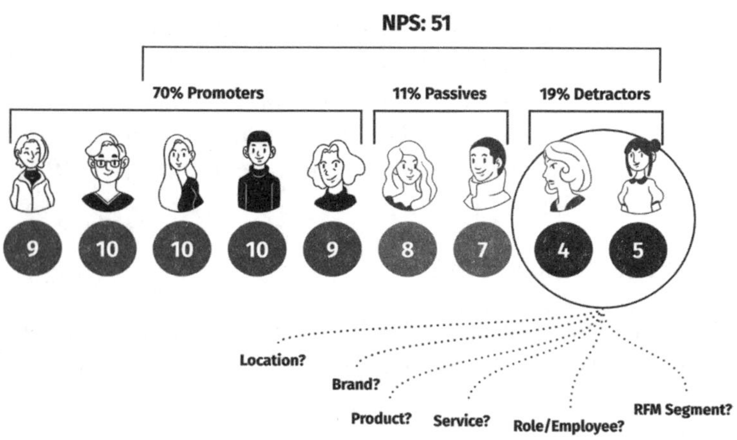

What's behind a Net Promoter Score of 51? The average does not tell you too much, except that things are not looking too good for this company. However, drilling down and looking at the NPS by RFM segment reveals much more:

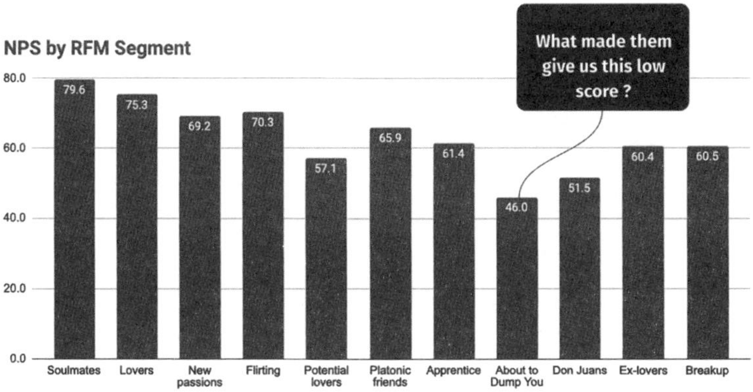

For instance, it shows that customers who are slipping away gave the lowest NPS score. This type of insight can (or should) lead to more exploration, starting with a simple follow-up question: "What made you give us this rating today?"

You might think it would be easier to simply give people multiple options from the very beginning. However, it's best to ask this type of open-ended question, then decide to offer your customers pre-built options. The reason is you don't want to guess what's important. You want to *know* from them what's important, then act on it.

With enough responses, you can begin to sort out the main themes. In the process, you will wind up with something like the following:

Reasons why they gave a low NPS	All the customers
Low Product quality	31.0%
Low Service quality	7.4%
High prices	14.1%
Slow delivery	4.7%
Delayed delivery	1.9%
Can't return the products	1.8%
Unresolved issues	2.4%
No discounts	5.7%
Bad employee attitude	4.1%
Low product diversity	2.3%

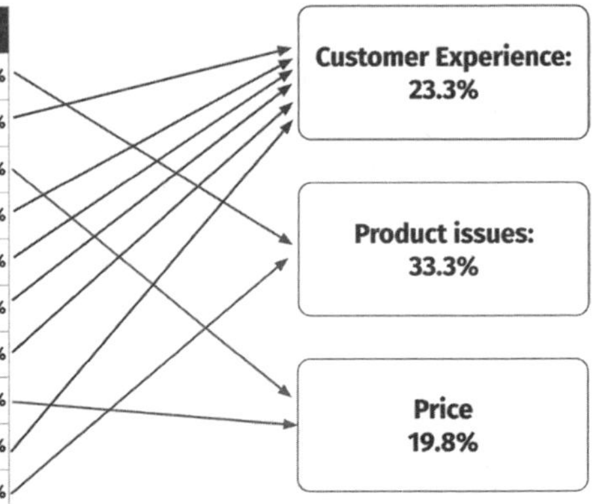

From there, if you want to drill down into each RFM segment, you can do so as well:

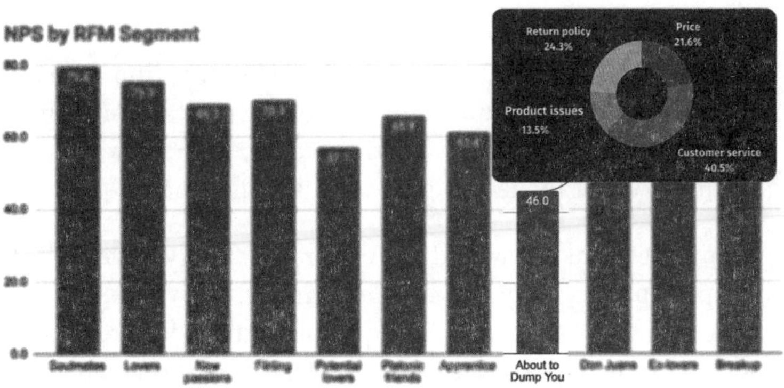

The purpose of this type of research is to come up with actionable insights, and (once again) to fix what's broken.

Turning Customer Support into a Profit Center

I want to share one more piece of the NPS puzzle with you, and that involves amplifying your customer support. A few pages ago, I mentioned our office supply customer with the staggering 92 NPS score. They consistently go the extra mile—ready to identify what might be going wrong and automate their support. Notice I wrote "what might be wrong," and not "what's going right." Good news feels great, but bad news is directive. Good news says "Hey, keep up the good work." Bad news says, "Hey, wake up and shake it up, before you're dead!"

My suggestion for serious customer-centric teams is to be accountable and actionable in the face of bad news. Don't be afraid when the data comes back and punches you in the eye. Take the hit, then plan your counterstrike. Here are six steps to help:

1. **Gather Enough Responses**

You need as many responses as possible if you want to identify the root causes of the low NPS scores. In order to get a statistically significant number, you may need to do the following:

- Test out different email subjects
- Repeat the number of messages you send out, and don't be shy about adding a little scarcity, such as "This is your last chance to share your opinion."
- Diversify your channels. You can run remarketing ads toward recent customers, send them SMS messages, or even call them.

2. **Monitor More Than NPS**

NPS has many friends and loves to play with others. Don't overlook different types of monitoring to support your NPS work, like CES (customer effort score), CSAT (customer satisfaction scores), and TTFR (time to first response), to name a few.

3. Focus on Main Issues

Something led to your low NPS score, to begin with. Work with the other departments to fix it. Then, once it's fixed, keep an eye on it. If the issue has happened once, it can happen again.

4. Set Real-time Alerts and Respond to Detractors

If you lack the resources to take care of every detractor, at least see if you can focus on staying on top of Soulmates and Lovers (and perhaps New Passions). Here's a glimpse at the tool we use to do so:

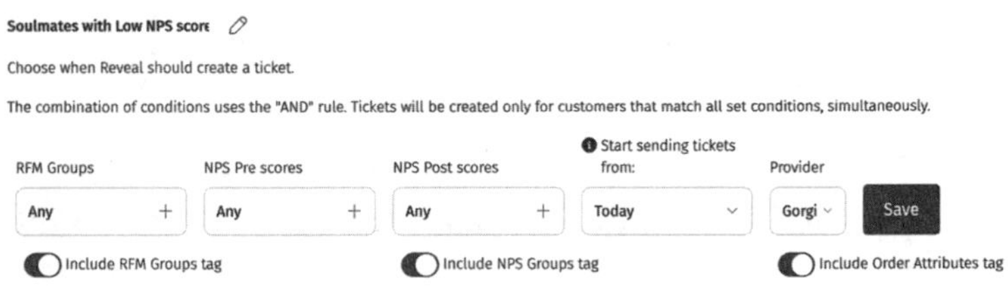

5. Build and Share Overview Reports About NPS

This will help make everyone aware of the status of your NPS. Is the NPS going down or up? Which are the best categories? What segments are giving us the highest NPS? How about the lowest? This type of insight can help dramatically increase motivation, accountability, and group cohesion.

6. Make Someone Responsible for NPS growth

Your NPS specialist can take the reins when it comes to putting together realistic targets for pre-delivery, post-delivery, and post-usage NPS scores. Of course, in order to improve it, this person should also come up with initiatives that will be implemented.

In the end, improving NPS is a bit like losing weight: You can't just measure the outcome (your weight). You have to track the work you put into losing weight: Are you exercising? Running? Walking? What about dietary changes? You have to count every contributing factor, for better or worse, and you have to be honest with yourself.

Alone, NPS messages and surveys make great ways to identify buying frictions. As data, they help you turn qualitative feedback into a quantitative number you can align with RFM segmentation and track over time. It's another powerful tool you use as you shift toward becoming a more customer-centric business.

Homework: Are You Customer-centric?

How customer-centric is your organization? Go online and take the CVO maturity assessment.

BIT.LY/CVO-MATURITY

With all of this focus on NPS and talk of customers, you might be itchy to get into the campaign initiatives. I promise that we are almost there. First, I'd like to focus on customer journey mapping, one of the final pieces to make sure everyone in your company aligns around your customers.

CHAPTER 7

Customer Journey Mapping

When everyone in your company aligns around the customers, it will start to feel like your customers are sitting in on strategy meetings. Leveraging the data and insights you gain from what we've discussed in chapters 5 and 6 (from Jobs to be Done interviews through NPS scores) will help you get closer to truly being a customer-centric business. These insights give you extra leverage for when you need to share hard numbers that show the good or the bad, especially in the face of organizational inertia.

To move the needle, you sometimes have to be able to change inflexible minds. This can be daunting if you're not the owner or working from the C-suites. Customer insights can help lead the way, and that brings me to the importance of customer journey mapping. However, before we go deeper into the business details, I'd like to share a quick story from the world of medicine and the early days of germ theory.

Causing (and Hopefully Solving) Your Own Problems

In the mid-nineteenth century, a Hungarian physician named Ignaz Semmelweis was one of the first in the field of medicine to apply the idea of antiseptic procedures, specifically hand hygiene. He worked in a Vienna hospital where many women were dying shortly after giving birth. There was a huge divide in the death rate among women who birthed in hospitals and those who birthed in the care of midwives.

Semmelweis set out to discover the cause and dove into the data. One of the first things he discovered was that in hospitals, the same obstetricians who facilitated births also performed autopsies. Often, they would go from one task to the other without washing their hands. Semmelweis saw the correlation. The doctors were spreading disease. They needed to wash their hands with an antiseptic, and the death rate would drop.

This might be a no-brainer to us today, but not so in Semmelweis' time. That was still the early days of germ theory. Talk about organizational inertia. Some doctors took offense to the idea that they were the problem.

Semmelweis died before his theory gained widespread acceptance. His theory is a good metaphor for what e-commerce professionals run into sometimes:

- He was the first to recognize a problem. (Many of us are in this boat.)
- He dove into the data. (Of course.)
- He developed a theory based on the data. (Yup.)
- He saw the benefits of change. (Been there.)
- He tried to get others to see the light. (Done that.)
- He ran into walls. (Ouch.)

Have you been in one of those meetings where you lay the data bare, but someone with seniority decides to follow their gut to (not) fix the problem? Maybe it's about their ego, or money, or a lack of resources, or they don't want to turn the ship around. No matter what prevents them from seeing the light, this mindset can lead to a painful trip to the boneyard of dead companies.

Customer Journey Mapping is a Strategic Steering Tool

When a company is struggling but not yet in a death spiral, they still have choices. One involves putting more trust in the idea that their customers might hold the key to helping them turn things around. The reasons why companies continue to de-prioritize customer insights or to overlook Customer Lifetime Value vary:

- Some lack knowledge about tools they can use to monitor CLV. (By this point in the book, this is not you.)
- Others are reluctant to listen to what customers are trying to communicate. (Also, not you.)

- Lots of companies forget or ignore the idea that people buy jobs, not products. (Still not you.)
- In certain cases, there's a lack of internal alignment that creates silos, organizational inertia, chaotic reporting, or another organizational challenge. (Hmmm....)

Are you familiar with the "rabbit-duck illusion?[3]" Check out this wonderful graphic:

Perceptions differ from person to person, even when they look at the same thing. When companies choose to move ahead without listening to data-driven insights, they're convinced that how they see things is true and that the numbers and feedback must be something else. They're dark about what customer journey mapping is and why it's important. This type of blindspot can get worse when people operate in silos:

3 The rabbit–duck illusion is a famous ambiguous image in which a rabbit or a duck can be seen. https://en.wikipedia.org/wiki/Rabbit%E2%80%93duck_illusion

- The customer service department collects useful data. Marketing chooses to ignore it.
- Marketing listens to data, but the sales department chases them away because the new messaging doesn't align with their strategy.

To become as customer-centric as possible, you have to analyze customer journeys and put the insights to use across every part of your company. That means marketing, tech, product development, CX, sales, and fulfillment must all dance together.

When you apply customer journey mapping, you improve results, especially if you're already focusing on CLV. As you get to know more and more about your Soulmates, customer journey mapping helps you create more relevant customer experiences for everyone.

If your customers aren't in love with your brand or products, your business will not scale effectively. You'll be putting gas into a broken car, wasting money while you get nowhere. Mapping helps you gain three critical insights, so you can speed down the road:

1. What is broken in the existing customer journey? Product? Shipping? Customer service? Marketing?
2. What do you have to do to fix what's broken?
3. How do you go forward once you've fixed it?

Customer journey mapping is not a one-size-fits-all experience. For example, let's say that "your gut" tells you to try a loyalty program. You decide to offer a 15 percent discount on purchases over $100. Perhaps this type of program will incentivize certain customers to buy again and others to buy more than usual. However, if you skip customer journey mapping, do you know that you're really giving customers what they want? What if you actually lose money because Soulmates were going to spend this much money anyway. Or, what if you blast this message to a bunch of customers who don't like your products?

Eliminate Friction Between Customer and Company Journeys

Sometimes, a company's journey does not align with the journeys their customers take. The company wants to sell products, while customers want to find solutions. To do so, they "hire" your products to perform the job of fixing their problems.

Customer-centric companies understand the dilemmas their customers face, and look for ways to move in this direction. They want their customers to know that they hear and understand them. Again, not all companies see things this way. This is especially the case when a company's view of metrics is limited to a narrow glance at P&L statements, much as we discussed back in chapter 1.

Within the CVO methodology, Customer Journey Mapping works best when you have eliminated silos, and follow a collective strategy whereby the journeys of your customers actually help steer your company's journey. This includes many of the touchpoints we've discussed throughout this book, as well as others:

- Gathering and sharing insights from customer research
- Financial modeling
- RFM segmentation

- Jobs to Be Done interviews
- Additional surveys that leverage JTBD results
- NPS scoring

Building a Customer Journey Map

A customer journey map shows the customer journeys over time. It illustrates the story of how your customers experience and interact with your company across any number of touchpoints (online, social media, email messaging, customer service).

Here's a visual example of a customer journey map, using a fictionalized online retailer:

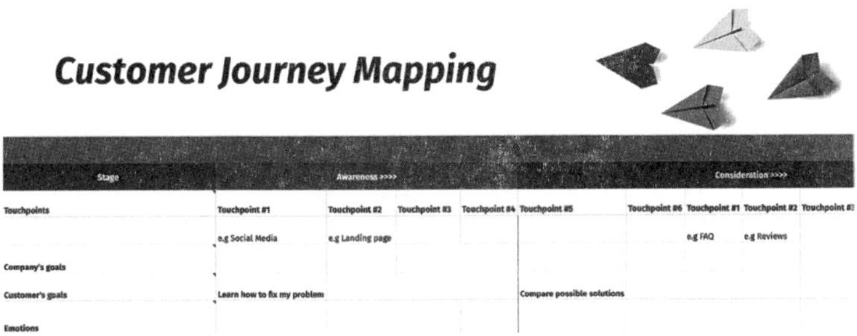

One of the most important aspects of Customer Journey Mapping is that the visual representation helps to keep your company accountable to all aspects of the customer experience. By now, you have gained many insights into various pain points and issues. The customer journey map helps you see and focus on solving them in order to enhance the customer experience. With so many touch points mapped out (web, social media, etc.), you have new access to understanding how, when, and why your customers are interacting with marketing, sales, fulfillment, and customer support teams.

Remember, this isn't a one-size-fits-all situation. The process will help you identify and map out experiences for various customer personas. Remember my firm's turmeric shot client from chapter 6? Here are some data points we extracted and focused on:

- Younger customers who used the shots for recovery and energy usually found out about them on social media, watched content on the company's YouTube page, then purchased the product through the online store.
- Older customers who used the product more like a daily vitamin usually read the company's blog, signed up for the newsletter, then tried it out. They were also more likely to refer friends and share content than younger customers were.

With this type of data, you can map out experiences based on various paths these customers follow. This helps you stay accountable to the needs and expectations of different customer-types.

In the end, mapping helps you step into your customers' shoes, and understand the journeys they take with your product.

- A visual customer journey map can make it easier for you to optimize future onboarding campaigns and efforts.
- Mapping is a great way to compare customers' pre-purchase wishes with post-purchase experiences.
- You can revisit customer journey maps when sales are slow, or if you notice a shift in issues, complaints, returns, or losses.

Before I wrap up chapter 7 and move into part 3, it's time to begin building your own customer journey maps. I've included a template that you can access and download from your dedicated CVO Revolution portal.

If you haven't visited the site in a while, here is the URL again:

BIT.LY/CJOURNEY-MAP

Once there, go to the video content and watch the short, three-minute demonstration about getting started with Customer Journey Mapping. To do so, you'll want to have your RFM segmentation and ideal customer profiles handy.

Your customer journey maps will be the final tools you'll need before we launch into part 3's campaign initiatives. Enjoy the process. When you're ready, let's begin putting powerful new initiatives to work, starting with acquiring new Soulmates.

PART 3

Act on Data: Initiatives that Matter

CHAPTER 8

That's how you take action

Repetition is the mother of learning. Let's start part 3 by recalling the three pillars of CVO:

(Is it burned into your head yet?)

By now, I bet you have a strong idea about how to fix and amplify the first two pillars from the left (What You Sell and What You Do). Part 3 is all about the third pillar (What You Say). Marking helps customers fall in love. When all three pillars are humming, first-time shoppers make the journey to becoming Soulmates for life. If you have followed the CVO methodology to this point, then you are on your way to making this so.

I must warn you that as you go forward, you might have to shift the way you think about marketing. There's a difference between focusing on sexy metrics around how many customers you acquire and fixing the entire customer journey by doing lifecycle marketing. The following visual will help you understand how to address each RFM segment with the help of six CVO initiatives: acquisition, onboarding, prevention, referral, loyalty, and reactivation.

	SOULMATES & LOVERS	NEW PASSIONS	APPRENTICE	NOT TO LOSE	ABOUT TO DUMP YOU	DON JUANS & EX-LOVERS	BREAKUPS
	Your best customers - loyal & active	New customers with high potential	New customers with moderate & low potential	Good customers that are at risk	Average customers that are at risk	Former best customers that are inactive	Former average customers
ACQUISITION	✓	✓					
ONBOARDING		✓	✓				
PREVENTION				✓	✓		
REFERRAL	✓						
LOYALTY	✓	✓		✓			
REACTIVATION						✓	✓

Six Types of CVO Initiatives

Chapters 9 through 14 will walk us through each type of CVO initiative. Before you and I explore them, chapter 8 is a cheat sheet to help start the conversation. Here's a high-level glance at certain aspects of the six campaign initiatives:

- In the beginning, your job is to acquire customers. You want your **acquisition** initiatives to be as strategic as possible. This will help you reel in high-potential customers (future Soulmates, Lovers, and even New Passions).
- Once you acquire them, you must ensure that they continue to get value from you and that your products do their jobs. Getting to the bottom of these details happens during customer **onboarding**.
- According to the purchase cycle, you have to prevent churn by making sure they are still getting value and will keep coming back with **prevention** initiatives.
- Once they are clearly happy with what they are getting, high-potentials become high-performers. You can count on them to help steer your acquisition initiatives, whether with word-of-mouth marketing, through JTBD research, or even with targeted **rewards** or **loyalty** programs.

- Will you lose customers? Of course. For times when these "naughty" customers fall out of love with your products (despite how awesome you are), you can prepare **reactivation** initiatives to win them back.

Depending on what your company sells, some initiatives are more important, impactful, and difficult than others. Take a look at the following graphic:

	Effort	Impact (based on the Purchase Frequency)				
		<1.2	1.2 - 1.5	1.5 - 2	2 - 2.5	>2.5
		Furniture, Mattresses	Pets, Consumer Electronics	Beauty & Fitness, Apparel	Toys & Hobbies	Food & Drinks, Books
ACQUISITION	HIGH	VERY HIGH	VERY HIGH	VERY HIGH	HIGH	HIGH
ONBOARDING	LOW	MEDIUM	MEDIUM	HIGH	HIGH	VERY HIGH
PREVENTION	LOW	LOW	MEDIUM	HIGH	HIGH	HIGH
REFERRAL	MEDIUM	MEDIUM	MEDIUM	HIGH	HIGH	HIGH
LOYALTY	MEDIUM	LOW	MEDIUM	HIGH	HIGH	HIGH
REACTIVATION	LOW	VERY LOW	LOW	LOW	LOW	LOW

It might help if you think of aspects of the customer journey like parts of a website funnel. To get more out of your optimization efforts, you have to focus on the most impactful areas.

The PECTI Framework

If you are really serious about embarking on a CVO endeavor (by now, you must be!) I have developed a prioritization methodology called the PECTI framework. It helps you invest resources as wisely as possible, as plot campaign initiatives. PECTI is a hybrid between CRO prioritization frameworks PIE (Potential/Importance/Ease) and TIR (Time/Impact/Resources). It takes into account 5 different criteria, rated from 1 to 5: potential, ease, cost, time, and importance.

THE PECTI CVO PRIORITIZATION FRAMEWORK

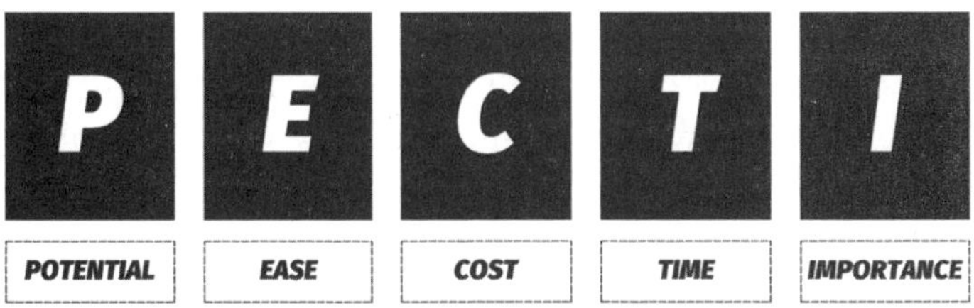

Your job is to score your optimization from one to five for each criterion, then decide your next steps. Here's a quick breakdown of the five criteria:

Potential

Estimate how much improvement you can make in various parts of the customer journey. Good thing you've been doing all your research!

Let's say you discover that the issue is CX-related. This means that putting focus toward your CX has the highest potential. Or, maybe your products have high net promoter scores, but you struggle to re-engage customers. Focusing on engagement has the highest potential, whether through marketing, product assortment, customer onboarding, or prevention initiatives.

Ease

Ease translates to how easy (or difficult) it will be for your company to make certain changes. Does it have the resources? How many departments need to be involved? Do you need more data? How will certain departments respond to changes? Knowing the ease is crucially important. Ease can bring you early wins, but the difficulty can quickly turn a smooth takeoff into an uphill scramble.

Cost

You cannot overlook costs. At the very least, you want to have a ballpark estimate of how much money will be involved. Is this a big commercial shift? What's the break even point of a loyalty program? Will you lose money since Soulmates were going to shop with you anyway? You can use CVO Academy's calculator tool to help you with the numbers.

Time

As always, time is of the essence. You need to take three aspects of time into account:

- How long will it take to start the activity?
- How much time will it take after launching to get noticeable results?
- How much time before you can set this change as a new *modus operandi*?

Beware you don't get too granular about things here. The point of the framework is to help you, decide which CVO initiatives make the most sense. Spend your energy on the initiatives, not on rounding time down to the nanosecond. Ballpark estimates are fine.

Importance

Importance means estimating the overall impact that activities within an initiative will have on the company as a whole. Know this first, then pump resources into it. In some cases, importance comes down to the customer segment you're addressing (Soulmates, Ex-Lovers, etc.). If the segment is massive and active, then importance will score high.

Here's an example of how a PECTI possible prioritization can look for a possible company. Mind the fact that these scores are not set in stone for those initiatives - they will vary from one company to another.

Potential CVO Initiatives	Phase	Potential	Ease	Cost	Time	Importance	Priority score
JTBD - based campaigns & onboarding	Acquisition & Onboarding	5	2	2	3	4	5.0
Real-time alerts based on the NPS scores	Onboarding & Prevention	5	2	2	3	4	4.6
Welcome back special treatment	Prevention & Reactivation	4	4	2	3	2	4.2
Adjust the follow-up cadence according to ADBT	Onboarding, Prevention & Loyalty	3	1	1	4	3	3.8
Surprise & delight with a package insert for New Passions	Onboarding	3	3	4	5	3	3.8
Prioritize the true gems products	Acquisition, Onboarding & Prevention	5	1	2	1	5	3.8
Win your wishlist - only if you place the 2nd order	Onboarding	3	4	3	2	2	3.1
Look-a-like ad campaigns based on Power Customers	Acquisition	2	3	3	2	3	2.7
Concierge follow ups	Onboarding, Prevention & Loyalty	4	2	4	1	2	1.9

Now that you and I have scanned the six types of initiatives, and explored the PECTI framework, let's dive deeper into each initiative, starting with acquisition.

CHAPTER 9

Start Strong, Be Memorable

Acquisition Initiatives at a Glance

Everything about Customer Lifetime Value begins with the acquisition. For almost all business models, acquisition initiatives have the highest impact. After all, no business can exist without acquiring new customers.

In Byron Sharp's book, *How Brands Grow,* he states how vital it is to acquire customers without worrying about only acquiring the right customers or channeling most of your marketing power towards retention. To a degree, this makes sense, even if it runs counter to the proposition I've presented in this book. If I've learned anything in my personal journey, it's to keep an open mind and avoid a fixed, overly dogmatic mindset about anything.

So let's unpack Sharp's view. No customer is truly a "forever customer," and it's a bit utopic to think that you can achieve zero-percent churn. Indeed, you need "fresh blood" to compensate for lost customers and achieve sustainable growth. Since churn is natural in any business, acquiring new customers is mandatory.

On the other hand, I am also a big fan of Peter Fader, one of the first people to demonstrate the impact of Customer Lifetime Value. His latest book, *Customer-based Audit,* demonstrates how and why companies must leverage RFM and fine-tune their acquisition towards the best customer segments.

Which way do we go? Do we follow Sharp? Fader? Split the difference? As with everything, I believe it's impossible to apply a one-size-fits-all approach. Still, there is a clear difference between being a small retailer and being a global brand. Knowing this difference and how it relates to your acquisition efforts can help light the way forward.

- A retailer has to play the game of product availability, diversity, and convenience. On the other hand, a brand has to understand the best jobs to be done with the help of its products.

- There's also a major difference between being an established brand and being the new kid on the block who has to penetrate the market.

Here's a little extra nuance to toss into the stew: When your resources are limited, as in the case of a new or small retailer, you can't afford to acquire too many low-value customers (unless you like losing money on acquisition costs). In other words, your need for economically viable acquisitions is higher than it is for established brands.

Orchestrating Your Acquisition Initiatives

There are many aspects to consider and questions to answer when it comes to orchestrating your acquisition initiatives and how much to invest. For example:

- **How mature or established is your company?** If you don't yet have product-market-fit, then you should think of your acquisition efforts as an experiment to validate or identify the JTBD. An ironic aspect here is that many established brick-and-mortar retailers don't have channel-market-fit on their digital channels, yet they pour a ton of money into the acquisition without fixing their business model first.
- **How important is purchase frequency in your industry?** If the average purchase frequency is greater than two, that means that having a purchase frequency that's less than two puts a customer in the bottom half of your RFM segmentation. There's no reason to continue to throw money at acquiring customers without knowing what makes your best ones come back or what products you should be replacing, eliminating, or adding to your offering. Here's a handy graphic to illustrate purchase frequency across a number of industries:

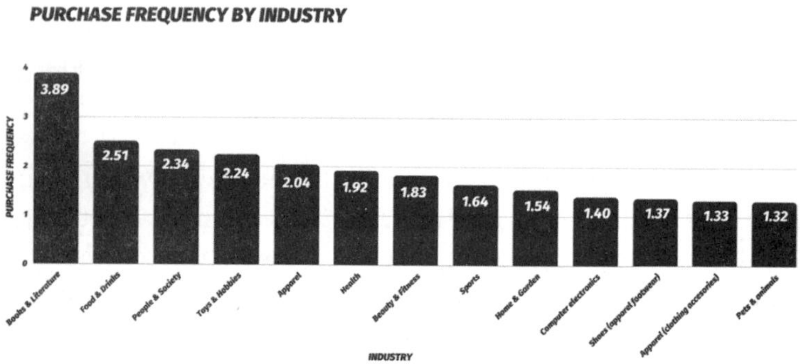

Source: https://bit.ly/CLV-benchmark

BIT.LY/CLV-BENCHMARK

- **What is your company's market share and market saturation?** There's a big difference between a recognizable brand that sells established products or being a start-up that sells newly emerged products. Are you a market leader or an upstart challenger?

Trusting Media Network

Can you rely entirely on what the media networks are telling you? Absolutely not. They are optimized to over-report their impact. This is also true for email service providers. Most of them use an inflated attribution window to get the credit they do not deserve. Here is a pro tip: Make sure you check the default settings when you adopt an email marketing solution. Likewise, can you rely entirely on what Google Analytics or advanced tracking solutions tell you? Not all the time. In part, the purchase paths are not always trackable. Customers are not always logged in, will use multiple devices from different connections, and frequently shop for others.

Post-purchase Surveys

You can always ask customers where they have heard about you. Start with an open-ended question, then expand the options to make it easier for them to respond and get a higher response rate. Can you rely completely on what the post-purchase surveys tell you? Not entirely. There are a few reasons for this:

- Respondents do not always behave like non-respondents. That's why they respond to surveys.
- The human mind is not always reliable. We tend to forget things. Plus, we're not always aware of the factors that may have influenced our purchasing decisions. Perhaps we overheard a conversation about a product two weeks ago, then saw an ad on social media a few days later, then overheard another conversation about the same product. Eventually, we decided to take a chance.
- It's hard to hope for true statistical significance early on. Instead, you should aim to gather enough responses in order to fill the pool before you swim into the data. However, this can be challenging, especially for smaller or understaffed companies. You need to aim to connect with people who exist on the other side of at least 10 percent of the orders. If you have only a dozen orders, that's not even a start. If you have a hundred orders, the number is too small. A thousand orders? Still too small, but you're getting there. This can lead to months of waiting.

- Not everyone that runs surveys knows how to craft the right questions to extract the truth. If you don't frame your questions properly, you could miss the whole point of the research.

Even with these issues in mind, a triangulation of these sources can still be more effective than blindly following an attribution model, which can be heavily biased. The idea is to make conscious trade-offs, optimize continuously, and revisit your decisions as you interpret and reinterpret the data.

BIT.LY/POST-PURCHASE-SURVEYS

Acquisition Does not Equal Growth

For years, e-commerce professionals have equated acquisition and growth as one and the same. As I have written, much of this is a result of a fixed mindset that says the acquisition is the only way to grow. Hopefully by now, you know of limitations to this type of thinking, and have discovered some critical aspects of acquisition marketing. Yes, acquisition marketing will always matter, but your mindset should not be "acquisition or lifecycle marketing." Instead, it should be "acquisition AND lifecycle marketing."

I never encourage businesses to move away from acquisition marketing. Instead, I want them (and you) to be as smart as possible about it. That way, as you acquire new customers, you create the right scenarios to invite them back. In the end, your acquisition dollars do not burn up in the churn but feed the furnace that keeps Soulmates and Lovers.

The acquisition will always be tied to growth, but the mantra of "acquire, acquire, acquire" is ill-conceived. With CLV at its center, the new mantra is "acquire, *inquire*, acquire." See what I did there? Inquiring into why your customers buy, whether you are reading the story of the data, or asking them directly, will help avoid churn and burn.

Just consider some of what you've already uncovered since the start of this book, with the help of the various pieces of homework and CVO-related tools:

- You know your best customers (Soulmates and Lovers).
- You know why they shopped with you for the first time.
- You know why they continue to buy.
- You understand the job or jobs your products perform for them.

Ideally, you've also learned a few things about gaps in your operations, issues you'd been ignoring, or even misconceptions from previous customers:

- Why did some former Soulmates stop buying?
- Was it because of problems with your products, marketing, shipping, customer service, or something else?
- Were your marketing messages misaligned with what they want or need or with their expectations?

With the sum of this knowledge, you can now focus acquisition initiatives toward attracting Soulmates and Lovers. At the very least, you know your acquisition campaigns will do the following:

- Start with the struggling moment or the pain points that people feel.
- Let them know your products are here to help.
- Address the "jobs" that bring the highest revenue.
- Or, narrow down to the top two jobs, and conduct AB testing at the start.
- Craft messages around these struggling moments.
- Amplify the first thought that customers have when they are frustrated with the thing they want to solve.
- Plant seeds for future purchases (a quick pivot toward onboarding messages).

Acquisition Initiatives Within the CVO Framework

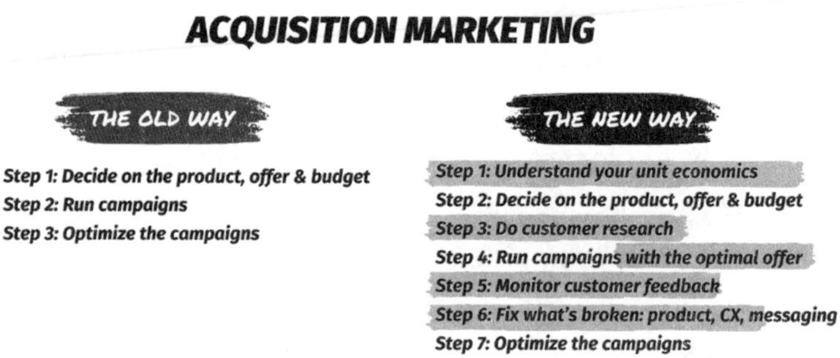

Let's get practical! Here are the steps to get you going smarter (not harder) with acquisition initiatives.

Step 1: Understand Your Unit Economics

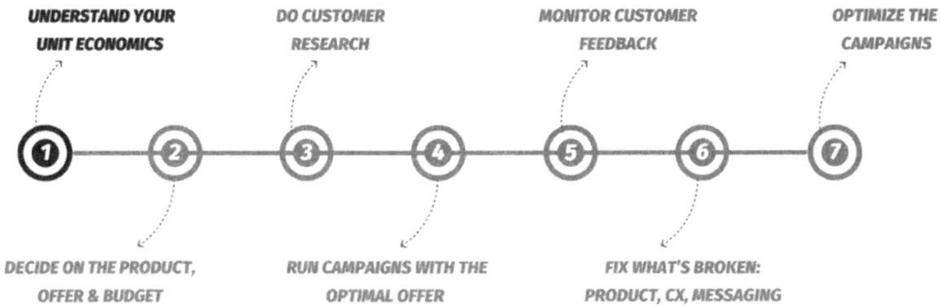

To begin, you must align acquisition to your unit economics. After all, you want to be profitable. Acquisition is great, but being profitable and increasing your company's value is even better.

Besides the dominant numbers that I explained in chapter 2, there are some other crucial numbers to be mindful of. For starters, how much can you earn from a newly acquired customer down the line, and how much can you afford to spend to acquire that customer? To uncover this answer, you must monitor the CLV to CAC ratio

For example, let's suppose you're selling coffee. For this particular customer, your acquisition cost was quite high. Let's say you paid $85 to acquire them, and after two orders (in two weeks' time), you have earned $66. You're almost $20 shy of breaking even.

Luckily, your coffee is a bio superfood, ethically produced by Maria José, a farmer from Guatemala, with an inspirational story you share on your website and packaging.

I have been in love with nature since I was 4. That's why I grow bio superfoods.

María José, Antigua, Guatemala

Thanks to Maria's story, your customer opens up your prevention email 35 days after the purchase. He buys it again. And again. And again. After five orders, your CLV to CAC ratio leaps forward, and you are earning a solid $2.12 in margin for every dollar you spend acquiring this customer.

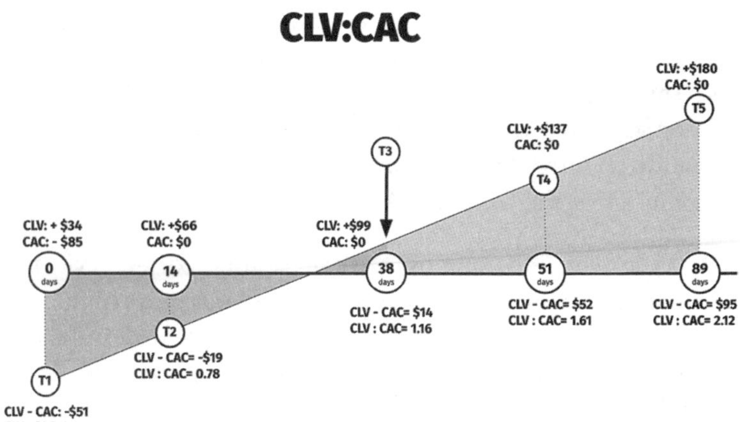

Now, once you have the CLV to CAC ratio calculated across your entire customer base, it's time to check how this looks for various RFM segments:

It will be an attribution nightmare to calculate the CAC historically by RFM segment, I suggest using <u>initially</u> a blended approach

RFM Group	All Customers	New Customers	Orders	Revenue	Margin	CRC (Customer Retention Cost)	CAC (Customer Acquisition Cost)	CLV (Customer Lifetime Value)	CLV: CAC
Soulmate	1,373	430	12,977	$1,268,069	$561,211	$16		$1,289	71.6
Lover	7,004	4,123	34,556	$3,268,380	$1,461,930	$14		$341	18.9
New passion	3,543	2,687	5,853	$543,831	$225,795	$12		$72	4.0
Flirting	11,164	3,867	13,377	$1,685,069	$691,335	$8		$171	9.5
Potential lover	4,748	2,877	27,078	$1,698,941	$712,362	$8		$240	13.3
Platonic friend	25,973	9,846	37,890	$1,697,844	$717,327	$10	$18	$63	3.5
About to dump you	55,565	37,325	83,245	$5,084,904	$2,105,976	$4		$52	2.9
Don Juan	13,255	11,345	13,255	$2,034,199	$838,026	$3		$71	3.9
Ex lover	14,848	4,866	26,784	$2,009,327	$842,824	$12		$161	9.0
Apprentice	26,768	24,586	26,768	$688,052	$278,636	$5		$6	0.4
Breakup	15,896	12,547	16,878	$421,732	$168,925	$2		$11	0.6
All	**180,137**	**114,499**	**298,661**	**$20,400,346**	**$8,604,346**			**$87**	4.8

Knowing these figures will already help you orchestrate better campaigns. However, you must calculate these figures across your entire customer base while keeping the break-even point in consideration.

For this, you must understand another vital metric: the CAC Payback Period. In a nutshell, the CAC Payback Period is the time it takes for your company to earn back your customer acquisition costs. If marketing and finance haven't collided yet, they're about to.

To calculate your CAC Payback Period, you have to understand what payback means. Let's look into various figures that should be connected with the reality of your company. First, as you probably know, one crucial element in the very real world of business is cash flow. Cash is the oxygen for any company. If your cash position is incredibly good, you can afford to invest long-term in acquiring customers. If it is not so good, you must acquire customers with as fast a turnaround as possible (turning materials into products; turning products into cash, as in the figure below).

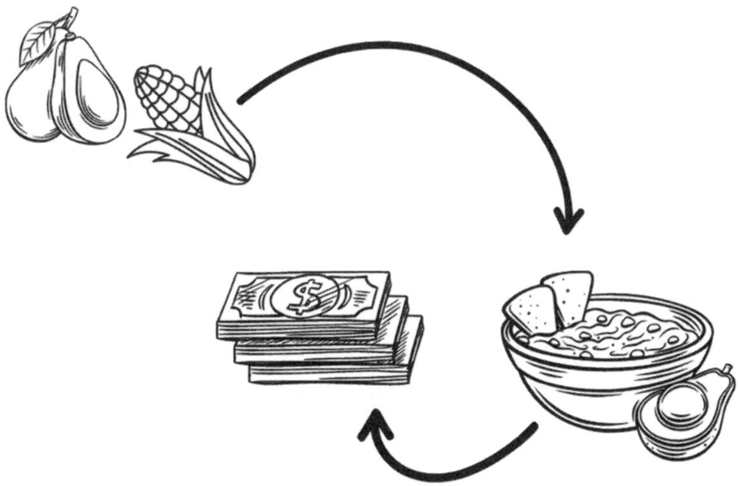

To stay cash positive, you must continue to understand your unit economics. Many companies calculate the CAC Payback Period based on revenue. This is misleading. I've provided two examples below to help demonstrate my point. In them, I have calculated the CAC and aggregated the data to show CLV across a series of timeframes: 30, 60, 90, 180, 365, and 730 days. Here is an example from a furniture store:

Furniture Retailer	Lifetime (days)	PF (Purchase Frequency)	CAC (Customer Acquisition Cost)	CRC (Customer Retention Cost)	CLV (Customer Lifetime Value)	Net Present Value (Cumulative, per period)	CLV per Day	# Days for CAC Payback
CLV-30	30	1.02	$122	$0	$609	$486	$20.31	6
CLV-60	60	1.05		$4	$659	$530	$10.98	11
CLV-90	90	1.15		$6.0	$763	$631	$8.48	14
CLV-180	180	1.20		$9.0	$844	$705	$4.69	26
CLV-365	365	1.25		$21.0	$891	$730	$2.44	50
CLV-730	730	1.30		$24.0	$963	$781	$1.32	93

The purchase frequency increases very slowly and gradually. After 730 days, the average number of orders per customer (frequency) is a mere 1.3.

In my second example, a grocery store, the situation is completely different:

Grocery Retailer	Lifetime (days)	PF (Purchase Frequency)	CAC (Customer Acquisition Cost)	CRC (Customer Retention Cost)	CLV (Customer Lifetime Value)	Net Present Value (Cumulative, per period)	CLV per Day	# Days for CAC Payback
CLV-30	30	1.26	$31	$0	$55	$23	$1.82	17
CLV-60	60	1.95		$1	$84	$51	$1.39	22
CLV-90	90	2.48		$1.6	$106	$72	$1.18	26
CLV-180	180	3.27		$3.6	$138	$102	$0.77	40
CLV-365	365	3.40		$3.7	$144	$105	$0.39	79
CLV-730	730	3.54		$4.9	$149	$104	$0.20	152

(I've included access to a template to adjust these figures for your own business at the end of this chapter.)

There are a number of other ways to go deeper into understanding and to level up your acquisition game by monitoring CLV by other attributes, including those I've listed in the graphic that follows:

CLV

- **BY CHANNEL** *(Facebook, Instagram, Affiliate, Organic Search, email, etc.*
- **BY LOCATION** *(New York, Bogota, Bucharest, Kinshasa, etc.)*
- **BY CATEGORY** *(Dresses, Skirts, Hoodies, Jeans, etc.)*
- **BY BRAND** *(Adidas, Nike, Puma, etc.)*
- **BY CUSTOMER SEGMENT** *(Soulmates, Lovers, New Passions, etc.)*
- **BY TIME INTERVAL** *(30, 60, 90, 180, 365, 730)*

To understand what you need to do, find the anomalies, then leverage them in your acquisition initiatives. But beware: while the Customer Lifetime Value to Customer Acquisition Costs ratio is a useful metric, you're still working with averages. To get even more granular, you must look for the actual details that live inside of your CLV to CAC averages. That's where breaking things down across variables (by channel, location, product popularity, etc.) becomes vital.

Step 2: Decide on Product, Offer, and Budget

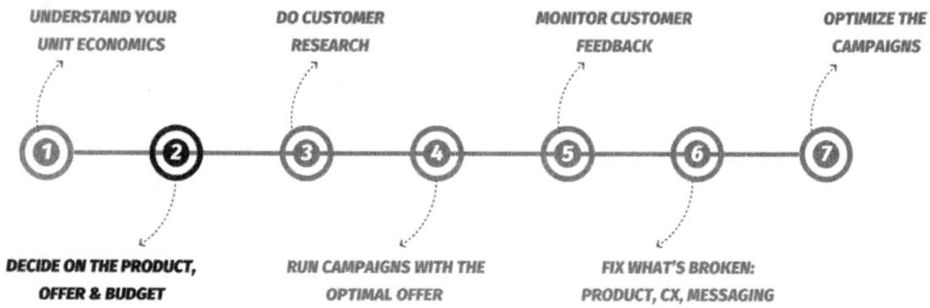

Traditionally, companies decide on acquisition limits broadly, simply by looking at an average and affordable cost-per-conversion, then considering their average gross margin. The current landscape is forcing us to be smarter, starting with the idea of being more than just spending managers. That's right: most marketing managers are "spending" managers when it comes to acquisition costs. However, when you leverage CLV within your acquisition strategy, the game changes. You begin asking new types of questions, like, "What is the maximum cost of acquisition marketing we can afford to use right now?" Indeed, you can forget minimums and work with bigger numbers. Here are some other questions you'll find yourself asking when you make this switch:

- How can we maximize our efforts?
- Can we invest even more in certain categories, brands, or locations?
- What do our customer journey maps tell us?
- Which "job" translates to the highest revenue?
- Where is the best place to put the majority of our acquisition spend?

What you find is that "spending more money" will quickly become "spending smarter money." In fact, when you sort out your unit economics, clarity becomes a brand-new superpower. You'll be doing the following in your sleep:

- Bidding differently to acquire Soulmates and Lovers since you already know that CLV to CAC ratio is much better when it comes to this kind of customer.
- Optimizing bids for ads on the products your best customers buy at the beginning of their relationship with you.

Step 3: Gather Customer Insights

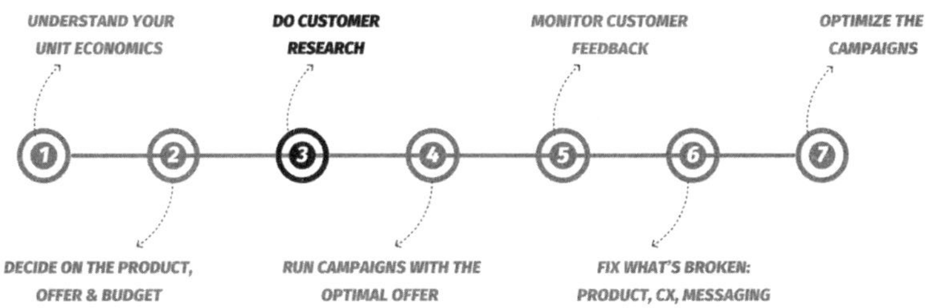

I hope you're not tired of reading about customer research and insights because here I go again. The reason I can't stop writing about it is that understanding your customers and what and why they buy gives you the ammunition you need to run the most effective acquisition initiatives ever.

Metaphorically speaking, your product is a bridge between a struggling moment and a desired outcome. You're not selling shoes, jewelry, soap, or oils. You're selling a solution, a job, a better way to live. You're selling a path that leads to a person's desired outcome. Is your product *everything*? No. But it is a part of the complete solution your customers crave.

With this in mind, you need to understand your customers' buying context in order to use the right messaging and position your product accordingly. Then you can run acquisition initiatives that truly make a difference. If and when you complete your customer research properly, your real customers will actually be the ones who write your ads for you.

Step 4: Optimize Your Offer

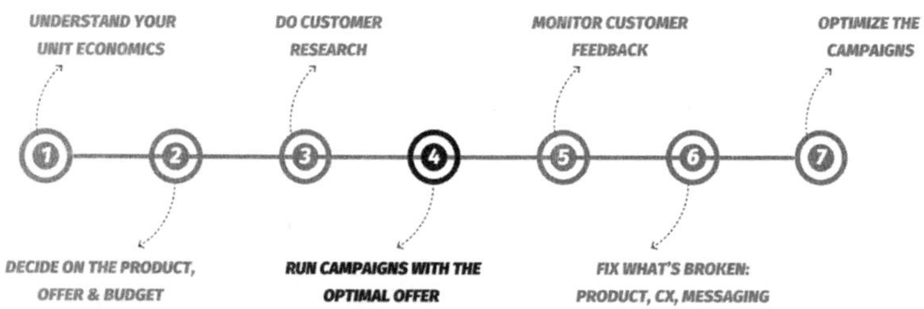

By the time you reach this point, you'll know the following:

- How much you can afford to spend.
- What products to focus on.
- What compelling messages to use.

With this information in your hip pocket, you are ready for what I like to call the "Holy Trinity" of acquisition initiatives. Namely:

1. Your offer (product, price, promotion)
2. Your target (by target I mean the channel & audiences)
3. Your creative execution

One catch is that most marketers jump straight to the creative, without doing the research involved in understanding how to craft it. I don't blame them for this. Most of them think that the algorithm will do the job. This is not the case (at least, not yet).

In order to pass the learning phase of paid campaigns, your messaging must be as compelling as possible. To create compelling messaging, you must know the struggling moments that get people to act (as I've written already). Having and using this information in your messaging helps you show customers the progress that your product will help them make.

Still, information alone is not enough. You need to spark emotions and access the mental structures that exist in their heads. That's why step 3 above is critical. Leaning into your research leads to higher engagement with ads, a faster learning period, a better algorithm, lower acquisition costs, and more Soulmates and Lovers among new customers.

Step 5: Monitor Customer Feedback

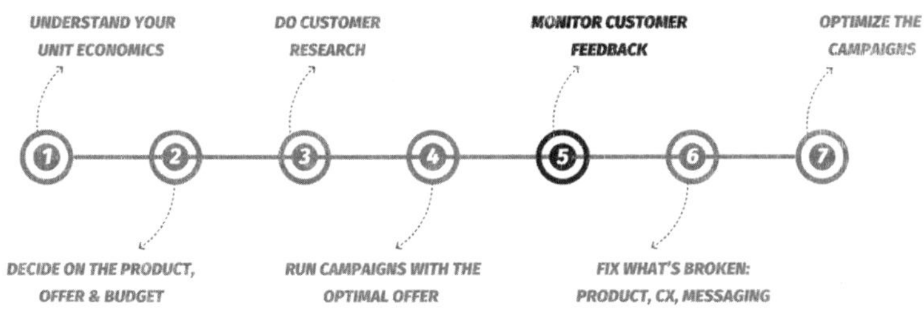

Monitoring customer feedback is the twin sister of gathering insights (step 3). The reason I want to include this step is to help keep your customer service team in sync with your marketing and merchandising efforts. If you ignore customer feedback, you are doing your business a major disservice.

This does not need to be rocket science. For instance, let's say you ask for the latest NPS and discover a detractor. This person happens to be a New Passion with high spending potential. What do you do?

If you only focus on the numbers, you might keep pushing the remarketing and acquisition pedal on them. However, if you listen to the feedback and you reach out to learn more, you might actually learn something. Perhaps with their help, you wind up eliminating toxic brands from your inventory or even just removing them from your offer. Or maybe you found out that there was some misalignment between the product and the CX. Whatever the case, the rule is the same: do not overlook feedback.

Step 6: Fix What's Broken (Product, CX, or Messaging)

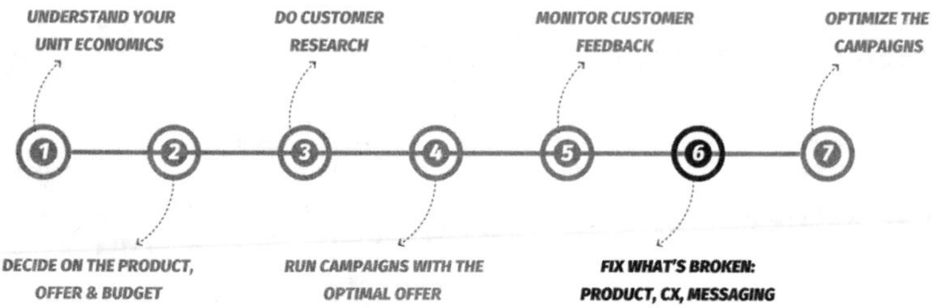

Step 6 follows straight out of step 5's focus on feedback. It also recalls something I shared earlier in this book: insight without action is useless. Getting feedback is great; not using it is not so great. Put the things that your customers tell you to use. This is not only about marketing, as it impacts your entire organization. However, things related to messaging, positioning, price, or inadequate targeting placements might change the way you make an acquisition. Incorporating customer feedback in your acquisition initiatives is a virtuous loop that never ends.

Step 7: Optimize Campaign Initiatives

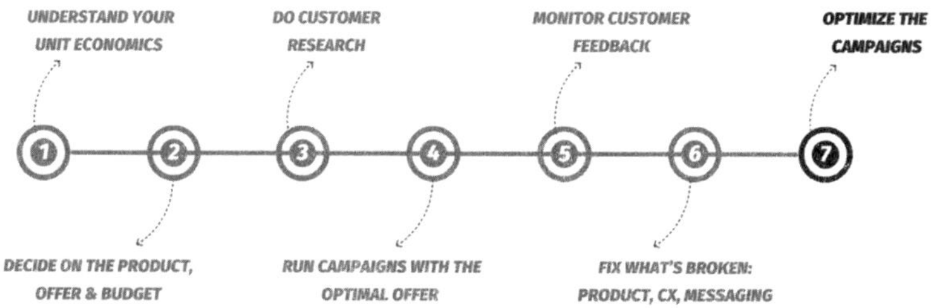

Our last step is another change to optimize. It's different from step 4. That step was about optimizing your offer, i.e., the message. Step 7 is about putting everything together in the most holistic fashion possible, including:

- Revisiting the steps you've followed to date
- Leaning harder into your data
- Reconsidering your message (offer)
- Listening to your customers
- Putting their feedback to use
- Rolling your campaign initiatives out even smarter than before

In chapter 5, I introduced something called the "4 Data Layers Product Optimization Framework." Optimizing your campaign initiative is an ideal example of putting the framework to use. (It's not a bad idea to re-read that section of chapter 5, especially as you prepare to blast out your new acquisition strategy.)

Using Seed Audiences and Zero-Party Data

There are a couple of ways to improve acquisition campaigns I want to share before I close out chapter 8. The first involves enriching the algorithm with seed audiences. To do so, you simply run acquisition initiatives by leveraging your best RFM segments (Soulmates and Lovers) to run lookalike campaigns. My company did this for ourselves and has built this in our Omniconvert offering for others to use. Our initial return was between 20 and 60 percent better than running standard new acquisition initiatives in social media ads.

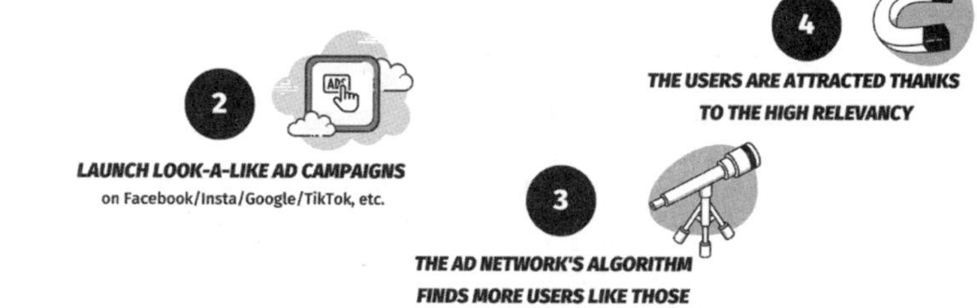

Seed audiences can also come from customers that bought from targeted locations or purchased certain brands or product categories. If you sell expensive sofas, for instance, you can't sell them again, but you can use the customers who bought them to feed the algorithm and then acquire more like them.

Another smart, data-focused technique to use to enrich these campaigns is to use zero-party data. This refers to information that customers intentionally and proactively share with your company.

The notion is to orchestrate acquisition initiatives that are relevant to these customers, based on how they recognize the struggle (assuming you collect them based on the JTBD), or the purpose of their visit. I'll explore this thought in greater detail throughout the chapters that follow, especially as you and I connect the dots between Acquisition, Onboarding, and Prevention initiatives.

An Acquisition Case Study

We worked with this customer for three years, a brick-and-mortar retailer that was heavily investing in growing the e-commerce side of their business. Their CMO hired us to help improve their website conversion rate. Before focusing on optimizing the CLV, our company was running CRO experiments. After dozens of successful AB testing experiments on their website and a pretty decent 31 percent win rate (the rate of winning AB testing experiments out of all the experiments), their CMO asked us for more help. They were facing massive competition from a new incumbent.

They were prepared to invest millions of dollars in a series of prime-time commercials in a large TV campaign. Their goal was to connect with the types of customers they perceived as their best: young urban professionals. When we asked how they knew who their best customers were, they responded that it was obvious on account of the demographics in their Google Analytics.

We had serious doubts about it. For one, not all visitors were customers. Secondly, not all customers were great customers. We did a deep dive into their data and conducted RFM segmentation research to find their ICP. We wanted to validate their intended direction for the TV commercials. In the process, we uncovered some critical elements that pushed against their assumptions:

1. Their best customers—those who ranked highest in RFM—did not live in large cities. Many came from either the suburbs or outlying areas beyond the burbs, but they did not land easily in the category of urban.

2. Their most loyal customers were not as young as the company believed. Rather than being in their late twenties or early thirties, the company's core shoppers skewed quite a bit older—the mid-forties.

3. We also discovered an important anomaly in their data: Most of their recently departed Soulmates had bought their new private label.

Imagine yourself in our shoes. The retailer hired us to improve their website ahead of a massive TV campaign. Here we were about to report to the CMO and CFO that their research was off, and they needed to adjust their strategy if they actually wanted to connect with soulmate-level shoppers.

In many traditional businesses with e-commerce wings, the e-commerce voices tend to get pushed aside when it comes to steering the ship. This is unfortunate since e-commerce professionals are the ones that have web and e-commerce data in their sights. Luckily for the retailer and us, we were able to leverage and present troves of data that said exactly who their customers were, why they were buying, and why they continued to buy. Here is some of what we presented:

- They lived in the suburbs, and the stores were an urban type of escape. They enjoyed the higher-end experience.
- There really wasn't another competitor that compared to the stores in the suburbs.
- They also enjoyed the clothing. They saw it as hip and sophisticated, a perfect blend of youthful and mature.

One of the many values of taking a CLV approach to acquisition strategy is that you can target by location, product, brand, buying source, or whatever you like, and pull more and more data from which you can focus your direction. As you adjust critical information in real-time, you effectively adjust your acquisition game as well.

Acquisition initiatives are high effort + high impact. It's a reminder of how much they matter and will continue to matter to the overall success of your business. In addition, The CLV Revolution acquisition templates are just that—templates.

We have designed them to help prompt some initial ideas. However, actual acquisition strategy and messaging should come from your research, feedback, JTBD interviews, the information you have pulled from NPS, and customer journey maps.

Get Started with Acquisition

Now that you're ready, go to your dedicated CVO Revolution portal, and download the acquisition templates to help you get started. Or, if you wish, continue onto chapter 9 first, and begin to build your customer onboarding strategy.

But before you go, I want to share the main benefits of applying the CVO method to your acquisition efforts:

- **Conscious budgeting:** When you know how much it costs to acquire a new customer and to recoup the cost, you can calibrate marketing and sales budgets so that you don't run out of cash and maximize growth. The indirect benefit of this is that your marketing manager and CFO will bury the hatchet (if one exists). Empowered with insight, people won't be worried about what you're spending to acquire customers.
- **Insight into marketing performance:** By comparing the CAC Payback Period over time, you can track the performance of various customer acquisition strategies, teams, and channels and determine what to bet on in the long run.
- **An optimized product assortment:** By comparing the CLV and CAC Payback by the first bought product, brand, or category, you'll know how to optimize your merchandise. You're right, that means more than the average CAC Payback period - you have to slice the data by the first bought product, but there are technology

providers that can do that if you know what I mean.

- **Cost savings:** Knowing how much to invest and the amount of time it will take to break even, your team can build promotion campaigns that actually work. No more "spray and pray" methods!

It's time to begin messing with the data yourself, with the help of the accompanying Google Sheet file here:

BIT.LY/RFM-TEMPLATE

Of course, you can also use properly designed and carefully crafted software courtesy of a team of professionals obsessed with CLV. Perhaps a little reverse psychology can help:

CHAPTER 10

Build Long-Term Relationships

Onboarding initiatives create a two-way communication, unlike acquisition initiatives which follow a one-way stream where you promise to meet their needs. Like a true conversation, onboarding is where you come to understand their motivations better, assess their frictions, and uncover any issues they run into when it's time to buy again.

As a customer-centric company, you shouldn't be trying to push products onto customers or coerce them into buying something. Your goal should be to make it easy for them to find and use products that help them make progress in their lives. That's the true path to building a community of Soulmates and Lovers who champion your brand.

Turn First-Time Buyers Into Soulmates

I hope that the changes you made to your acquisition campaign strategy following chapter 8 worked. Now it's time for onboarding initiatives. The onboarding phase has one single goal: Make sure that customers extract value from the products they bought from you. To achieve this, you have to find the right way to tell your customers that they are your top concern and that your main interest is to make sure they are happy. When you show them you're paying attention, you will set the groundwork for keeping them around and help them find reasons to shop again. Maybe they'll even tell their friends about your business.

Here's a scenario many of us have been in: We buy a pair of shoes online, then are instantly bombarded with discounts and remarketing ads and emails to buy another pair of shoes. Worse, these messages start hitting our eyeballs well before we even receive the shoes we bought. The company doesn't even know if we've received the, or if we'll ever receive them, never mind how they might look or feel.

This situation demonstrates a simple and unfortunate truth: the company in question doesn't care about us, just about making money. Where does this lead? Take a look at the chart that follows:

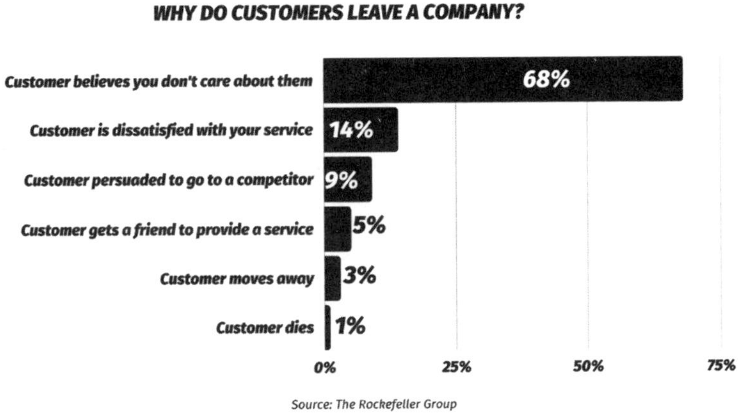

The top reason why customers don't buy again is due to how they perceive a company. If they feel like the company doesn't care about them or isn't interested in their customer journey, that's more than enough for them to walk away.

Knowing this, the onboarding phase must start well before customers receive the products from their first purchase. You begin planting seeds the moment you communicate the product's benefits, then continue with how you set expectations all the way through your thank-you-for-your-purchase message.

The more you show customers that you care about who they are, the higher the chances they'll settle into a solid buying habit. Once again, a lot of this depends on how well your product or service helps them move forward in their lives.

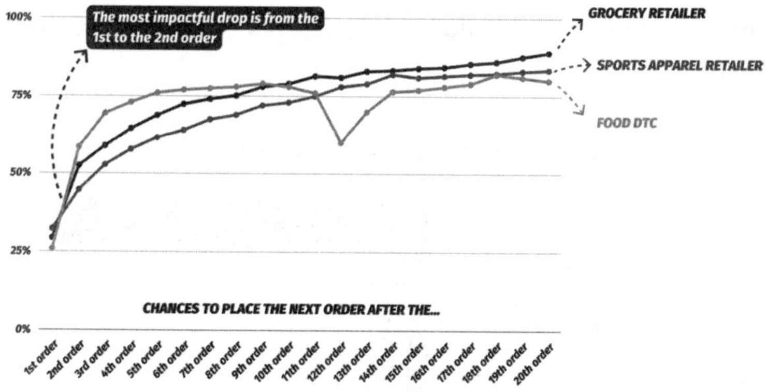

As the chart above shows, the chance that someone places a next order grows as customers place more orders, the drop at month twelve for the Food DTC notwithstanding. Depending on what you sell, you can consider a customer's onboarding phase to be finished after the chance to place the next order peaks and continues to trend above 70 percent. This shows that your store has achieved first-to-mind status for most customers.

Being First-to-Mind

Consider a trip to your local supermarket. If you're already loyal to a certain yogurt brand, for instance, you simply pick it up, put it in your basket, and continue down toward the eggs. That's not a buying decision, it's a buying *habit* that you make without too much awareness or consideration. You've already picked that product; paying for it is simply a formality. This is what it means to achieve first-to-mind status, and it is one of many gifts that come on account of a successful onboarding phase. It signals that a customer is even more likely to place their next order than they were to place their previous one.

Customer vs. Company Journeys

If you look at how most retailers handle the onboarding process, you realize there's a huge disconnect between customer and company behavior. Here's a real example:

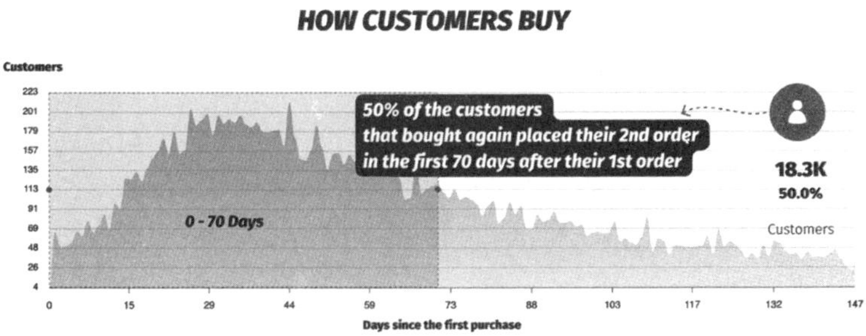

Remember the average days between transactions (ADBT) from chapter 2? I first mentioned it when I wrote about the difference between traffic and customers. Look what this chart shows about customer purchasing habits after their first purchase and the number of days between first and second purchases. With this in mind, let's see how this company communicates with its customers:

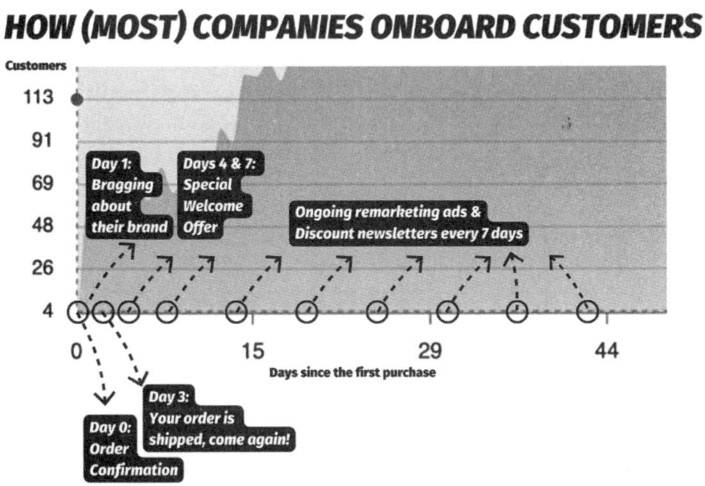

among many online retailers. The irony is that marketers who orchestrate these campaigns are customers too. Even though some of them realize how ineffective this approach is (they have themselves as data points, after all), they continue this vicious cycle. Why? Mostly because they see it as being "good enough."

Now, let's see how it looks when done properly. First, let's go through some of the questions customers ask themselves after placing a first order:

- Was this a good decision?
- What if they don't send me the product?
- When will I get it?
- Can I return it if I don't like it?

Customers have all sorts of reactions after placing an order. Many go through what's called "buyer's remorse," a sense of regret after a purchase. Perhaps you have been down that road yourself.

A company must address this. In the process, they must decrease an important KPI: product return rate (PRR) that harms revenue. To do so, they must offer clarity, answer unaddressed questions, and get ahead of any potential objections before they appear in a customer's head. The following graphic shows provides a visual of how this might play out:

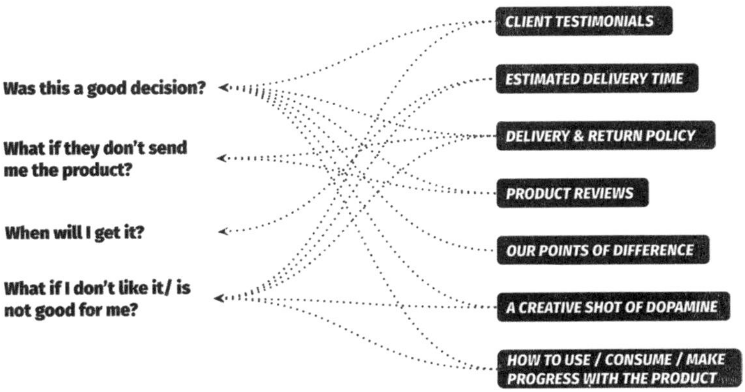

A First Time, Then a Series of Next Times

When a person makes their first purchase, they're not buying a product—they're buying the idea of what that product will do for them. These new customers have even paid in advance for the idea of having your product in their hands. Now it's time to point them in the direction of making steady, ongoing progress in their lives.

Onboarding initiatives are about more than marketing or trying to generate "the next" sale. Yet far too many businesses go back to the drawing board and attempt to make more sales from the same source. They'll offer discounts, coupons, BOGO opportunities, and refer-a-friend campaigns, all in the hopes of incentivising another purchase. When companies do this, it comes across like they're only interested in pushing products. A customer-centric onboarding initiative focuses on setting expectations about how the customer's life will change because of what they've already purchased.

CVO Onboarding for Brands

For established brands, onboarding campaigns are a way to check your customers' pulse. Do they like what they purchased? What NPS did they rate it? Are they interested in sharing more feedback via a longer survey?

For brands, the CVO onboarding process is all about helping people make progress in their lives. Your main focus should be to make sure they are using the product in a way that helps them achieve their desired outcome.

- Have you built your onboarding efforts around helping customers make progress and moving away from their struggling moments?
- Or, are you trying to push them toward their next purchase?

Remember, the relationship with clients can be fragile after their first acquisition. You don't want to push them toward the next purchase unless you know they are happy already. Remember, with lifecycle marketing, you must begin with the end in mind. For a brand, this means validating the jobs to be done, as well as the desired outcomes customers want. This involves leveraging your JTBD research in the onboarding experience.

This brings up a critical point: JTBD changes from acquisition to acquisition. The reason behind a customer's first purchase isn't going to be the same reason behind their second, third, fourth, or however many purchases come in the future. The following graphic provides a visual example of how JTBD research can unfold over time, even with the same customer:

JTBD ACQUISITION & ONBOARDING PROCESS

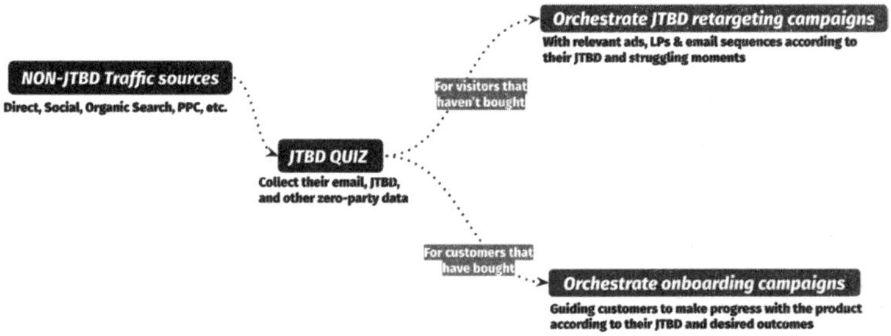

- With traffic that's already coming your way, you can trigger an interactive quiz to tag users according to their JTBD. Once you do this, you will be able to push more relevant email and ad campaigns to convert them and orchestrate more relevant onboarding flows according to the progress they are trying to make.
- With traffic you generate via specific messaging and creatives, you can craft landing pages according to each job-to-be-done.

JTBD ACQUISITION & ONBOARDING PROCESS

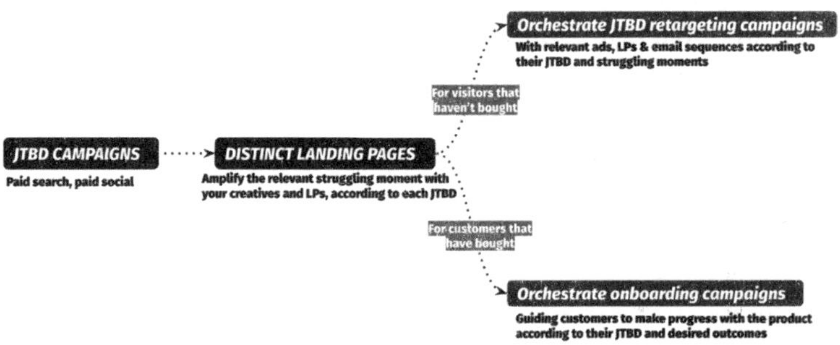

You can access a more detailed version of this process with the QR link below:

BIT.LY/ONBOARDING-FLOW

CVO Onboarding for Large Retailers

If your retail business sells hundreds or thousands of SKUs, you probably can't afford to leverage JTBD and adapt your messaging and onboarding according to every product's purpose. However, you can identify products that customers purchase again and again, which I wrote about in chapter 5. With this insight, you can build targeted onboarding initiatives that focus on motivation, ability, and the triggers that encourage people to stick around and shop again.

Removing friction is one of the keys here. It's easier to remove friction than it is to increase motivation. In this case, the friction or frictions you're removing as a retailer, are the blocks or walls that get in the way of the next purchase. A practical example is to let customers opt-in to a refill and ship feature that automatically replenishes their favorite products on a regular basis, according to their shopping and consumption patterns.

For many large retailers, onboarding initiatives focus on two types of new customers based on RFM: Apprentices and New Passions, with New Passions making a bigger splash during their first order.

	APPRENTICES NEW CUSTOMERS WITH AVERAGE POTENTIAL	NEW PASSIONS HIGH POTENTIAL NEW CUSTOMERS
	R: High F: Low M: Low - Medium	R: High F: Low M: High
ONBOARDING INITIATIVES	✓	✓

You can address these customers as one group (i.e., "new customers"). However, once you have about four thousand shoppers in the "new customer" category, you can split them into two segments and craft unique onboarding messages.

For example, if an Apprentice has a predictive CLV of $85, and a New Passion's is $344, it's all a matter of building a mathematical model and getting creative with what you offer as an onboarding incentive. Your goal is to find the right moment to trigger these onboarding initiatives and reach the break-even point based on the predictive CLV.

I'll share one last for large retailers. You can explore ways to integrate your onboarding strategy with product fulfillment according to each job-to-be-done. After all, there's one type of initiative out there that comes with a 100 percent open rate: the unboxing initiative. Your customers are going to unbox their products when they arrive. Consider using old-school packaging inserts to help them learn more about the product that's in the box, discover ancillary products that can also help them, or maybe even tell them all the ways you put their money to use as part of your company's give-back programs.

An Onboarding Case Study

One of our more unique clients in recent memory sold paint-by-number sets for adults. Via JTBD interviews, they uncovered some of the core motivations of their soulmate customers:

- Stress relief
- Relaxation
- A creative outlet that did not require much thought

Even before they completed RFM segmentation or conducted JTBD interviews, they were well aware that a large percentage of their repeat customers dropped off after purchasing a second painting set. Why would this be? As we discovered, they weren't having issues with the product or the company. Instead, the issue was with themselves: They simply weren't finishing the second painting and decided not to buy a third until they finished the second. It was a mental hurdle that customers needed to get over.

Working with the information we pulled together, we launched an onboarding campaign that would help solve this obvious challenge by encouraging customers across the finish line. Some of the tactics we used included sending check-in type emails written in a tone similar to a very supportive friend or performance coach. We also asked them to rate how they felt when they started a painting, when they were halfway through, and when they finished. Overall, the tone was passive but extremely positive. The main goal was to plant the seed of a future reward—buying a new painting set for themselves.

The most important takeaway from this example is that you can't say a customer has been onboarded if he or she hasn't actually consumed or used the product.

Now that we have unboxed our onboarding initiatives, let's take a look at prevention and the steps to take to keep customers from disappearing for good.

Get Started with Onboarding

Is there going to be homework, or a call-back to the CVO portal?

It's a bloodbath in the e-commerce landscape today. Providing a seamless onboarding experience can make all the difference in acquiring and retaining customers. If you work for a DTC or a brand, applying the JTBD methodology to your onboarding process, will help you gain valuable insights into the actual struggles of your customers - that leads to an unfair advantage against companies that provide standard, boring, and impersonal onboarding experiences. If you work for a retailer selling many SKUs, I urge you to take a closer look at your onboarding process and consider implementing a customer-centric approach you'll create a more engaging and satisfying onboarding experience that leads to long-term success. So take the next step and do your homework - find the link to the onboarding flow above.

CHAPTER 11

Stay Engaged

Just because a customer hasn't purchased in some time doesn't mean they're already lost. Prevention initiatives help you engage with people who may have disappeared, so they don't completely forget about you. Prevention initiatives are reminders that sometimes life happens, and customers go away for one reason or another. In some cases, it has very little to do with your company or your products.

Even the most successful companies out there are great at ignoring prevention altogether. However, these are potentially more impactful than reactivation initiatives (chapter 14), despite the fact that there are more customers that are already lost (Breakups, Ex-Lovers, and even some Don Juans) than customers that are about to churn (from the Not To Lose and the About To Dump You segments).

	NOT TO LOSE GOOD CUSTOMERS AT RISK	ABOUT TO DUMP YOU AVERAGE CUSTOMERS AT RISK
	R: Medium F: Any M: High	R: Medium F: Low - High M: Low - Medium
PREVENTION INITIATIVES	✔	✔

Prevention is the Best Cure

There's a saying in health care that prevention is the best cure. In the world of life cycle marketing, prevention initiatives can be pretty lucrative. They don't require much effort and can yield a high impact.

Prevention initiatives focus on customers who have started to slip away. You've already onboarded them, and they used to buy from you regularly. They used to be Soulmates or Lovers, but now they're in your RFM's "danger zone." It's time to build a prevention strategy that rekindles the magic.

Recency is the Trigger

A dip in Recency is the key to triggering a prevention intervention. You want to set up various parameters ahead of time to catch these customers before they disappear forever.

These should relate to specific purchasing criteria that align with your business and how your best, most active customers shop. Have more days passed between their most recent orders than previous orders? How many?

Prevention must not overlap with other ongoing or one-time campaigns. If you are triggering a prevention email sequence, make sure your messages are consistent. Don't send a personalized message or incentive one day followed by a general, non-specific message the next.

Knowing Why People Leave

These customers had been purchasing from you fairly consistently, but then their recency dropped off. Something has changed. What? Why? The goal of prevention is to create and communicate a relevant trigger that increases their desire to buy again.

Plenty of companies still bombard customers with newsletters, new releases, coupons, specials, limited-time free shipping offers, you name it. There's nothing wrong with using certain "teasing campaigns" within your overall strategy, but they are not the same as prevention initiatives. Prevention makes things more personal. Many successful prevention initiatives strike a tone that's similar to onboarding. You're not going for the next sale, but to keep the connection.

Another point to keep in mind has to do with preventing the drop-off before it happens. How can you do that? Churn is natural at different and difficult times, especially when customers are facing financial or personal issues. Prevention initiatives are most effective when you apply customer research to understand why customers are churning.

There's only so much that a company can do when a customer is going through a situation that affects how they spend money. Still, there are ways to listen, to stay informed, and find out if there's an issue between you and your core customers. It reminds me of a quote I've heard, which is often attributed to Desmond Tutu:

> "There comes the point where we need to stop just pulling people out of the river. We need to go upstream and find out why they're falling in."

If you continue to trust your research and data, you can piece together the reasons why even core customers are leaving, especially if you notice a dramatic drop in recency across a large group of customers in a short period of time.

With this insight at your disposal, you can effectively get ahead of your retention strategy and trigger a series of "check-ins" that build around the two-way conversation you've already built with these customers. Here again, the tone is similar to onboarding: friendly, helpful, and geared to help customers get more out of your products, as well as other resources you offer.

You lock this parameter into how you connect with top-tier customers. Then, toward the end of the 61-day window, you send a simple reminder: Is it almost time to restock? Perhaps you only send this message out after you reach day fifty-five. It's a simple nudge that can provide the effects you need.

What happens if a Soulmate doesn't purchase within the sixty-day window? Perhaps on day seventy, the prevention initiative begins. The messaging can shift away from the next purchase and toward something else as a way to keep them engaged. Perhaps you highlight a new product or offer access to new resources. The goal here is to keep them engaged and to remind them that you are here.

At the end of the day, if you have been relying on data all along—from RFM segmentation, through NPS and customer journey maps—then you should have a good idea of who your top customers are, as well as why they suddenly fade away.

Was there new friction in their customer journey? For instance, did they have a bad experience with your company recently? Was shipping delayed? Was there an issue with the packaging? You can gather this type of information with the help of simple email surveys after every purchase.

If there was friction, and they share this with you, it's your company's job to remove the friction. When you do, you increase their ability and willingness to buy again.

Prevention Actions

In the end, your prevention activities can become evergreen. Every time a customer starts to slip away, you can trigger the same rollout and take action. Here are a number of prevention actions to follow and keep in mind, based on the reasons why a customer is slipping through the cracks:

1. **Fix What's Broken**

You can set this type of prevention action to auto-pilot with real-time alerts that align with and leverage changes to NPS. See the diagrams below:

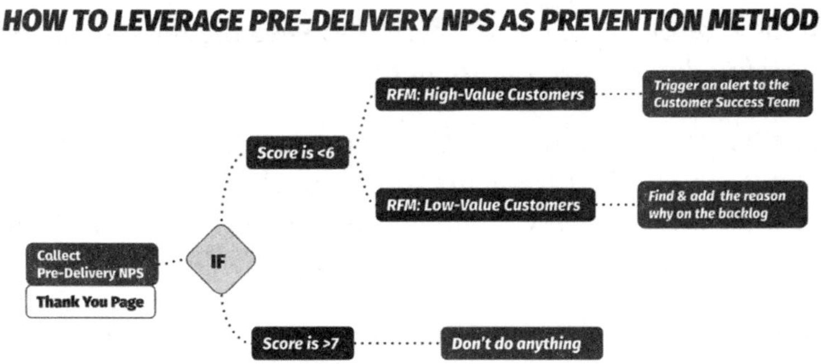

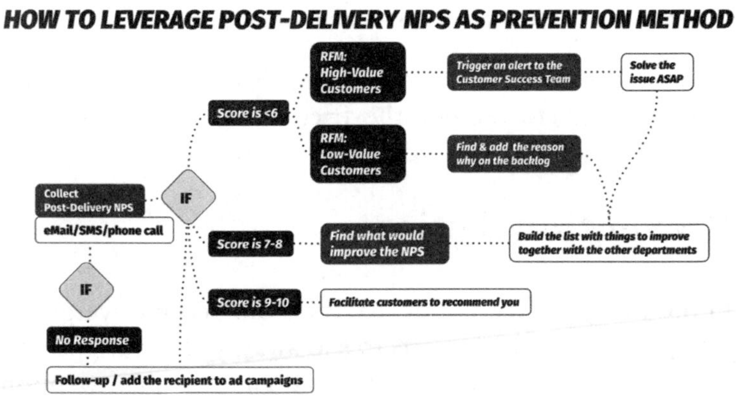

2. Adapt Your Messaging

Once you launch a prevention initiative, you'll want to verify the transitions between RFM segments, check the impact of these changes, and then adjust. Here, optimization means launching experiments and learning from every move you make.

3. Inspire without Bribing

The best prevention make customers want to come back without a bribe. That means you have to find relevant and creative ways to make them want to hear from you. Knowing what kind of progress they're trying to make with your products helps.

Here are a few softer, non-commercial ideas to work into your messages that can help prevent customer churn:

- New collection announcements
- Updates about products they've purchased before or mentioned in a "wishlist" they may have shared during the onboarding phase
- Replenishing emails that include restock and refill reminders
- A note about their loyalty points (more on this in chapter 12)
- Last chance messages when certain products are low in stock, or products that you will be phasing out from your catalog
- A note about favorite brands (based on feedback)
- Sharing success stories about people who benefit from the same products these customers buy and use
- A creative series of "thank-you" notes within package inserts

A Prevention Case Study

Sometimes, the friction that prevents a person from purchasing again is deeply personal and has nothing to do with your company. A story that comes to mind involves an online retailer that sold an assortment of treats and other pet supplies, mainly for dog and cat owners. They were already extremely personable in how they connected and supported their customers. They knew that they needed to be delicate whenever recency dropped off; in plenty of cases, it was because of the death of a beloved pet. Therefore, they couldn't simply bombard their soulmates with "where have you been?" messages.

Still, they understood the importance of staying in touch and did not want to completely disappear from the lives of these customers. How could they walk the line without overstepping a boundary?

One of the most powerful parts of the client's business model was their customer service department, many of whom were pet owners themselves. These professionals were on the front line of connecting with customers.

One of the first places we encouraged them to focus was on making sure they were putting this data to use. Their customers were often very forthcoming about the age and health of their pets. The company began to put more attention on candid phrases that customers shared in emails and messages, things like "my dog is getting up there," "my cat is a senior now," "she's been feeling run-down lately," and things like that.

The company updated its prevention strategy to include occasional check-ins that came from customer service. The intent was simply to stay in touch, with a very personal and personable tone: "We wanted to check in and see how things are going with your pet." Sometimes, these messages included special offers, in addition to links to other products for senior pets (blankets, cuddle toys, posturepedic beds, pill pockets, soft treats).

Even in cases where former soulmates stopped purchasing completely, these types of check-ins were valuable for the brand. They helped to communicate a new level of care and compassion, so when soulmates became pet owners again in the future, they didn't hesitate to return.

Get Started with Prevention

I invite you to visit your dedicated CVO Revolution portal and download the prevention templates. As with the acquisition and onboarding homework, the prevention work will help to prompt your initial ideas. As you design (or redesign) your prevention strategy, keep in mind that timing is one of the most critical aspects you'll need to identify and decide on.

- What is your "magic" recency number?
- What steps or messages do you want to take as this number gets closer?
- What type of message or group of messages do you want to send out after a soulmate shoots past this number?
- How many days must pass before a customer moves from prevention to reactivation? You can determine this based on the Recency score. Customers that need to be reactivated have the lowest Recency score.

Want to go more in-depth with the prevention campaigns? I have crafted a mind map that's emphasizing how your company should behave at various key moments that can be set as triggering events for various actions:

- When the customer is placing the first order
- When the customer has contacted your customer support

- When the customer is on your website before receiving the first order
- When the customer has received the first order

You can find it here:

BIT.LY/POST-PURCHASE-FLOW

Next up, let's take a look at ways you can create more customers with the help of your existing soulmates, via referral initiatives.

CHAPTER 12

Referral Programs

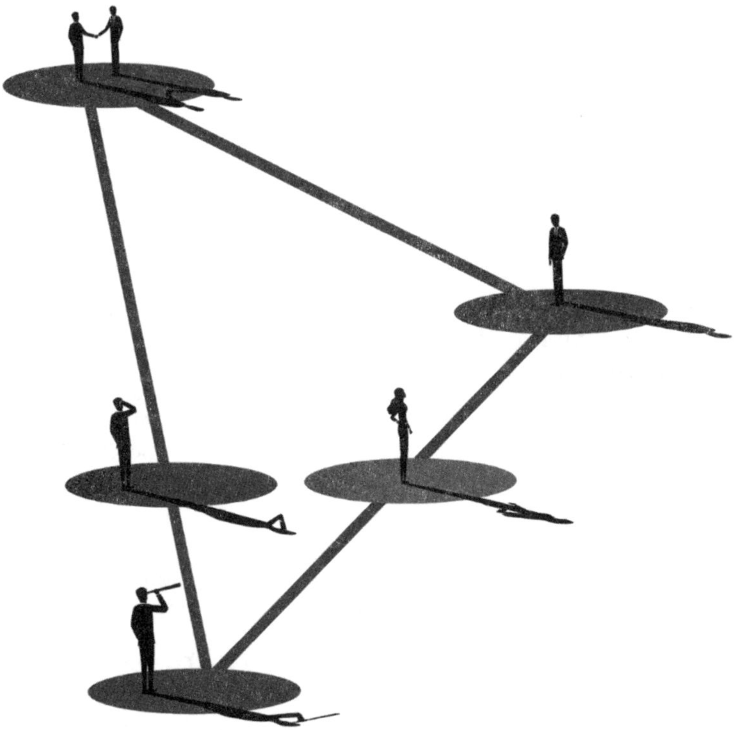

It's possible that your loyal, soulmate customers will love your products or services so much they might even become cultish about your brand. Naturally, this can be a very good thing. Such conditions are ripe to create referral programs.

In chapter 6, I introduced you to the advanced e-commerce Growth Flywheel. Here it is again to refresh your memory:

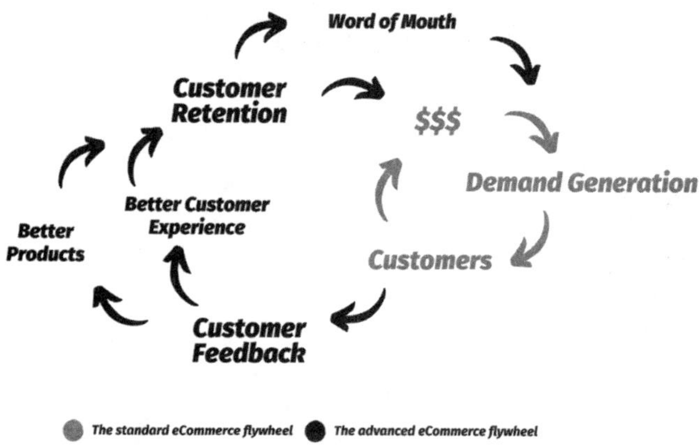

Word-of-mouth marketing is a great way to generate demand without paying for ads. As you improve customer experience and continue to sell amazing products that fulfill their jobs, you increase your chances of generating word-of-mouth referrals. Still, let's not ignore the question on the table: Do referral programs actually work? Here are some proof points from a few sources:

- Referred customers have a 16 percent higher lifetime value compared to non-referred customers.[4]
- Referred customers are 18 percent more likely to stay with a company for longer and are 16 percent more profitable than non-referred customers.[5]

4 Schmitt, Philipp, Bernd Skiera, and Christophe Van Bulte. "Do Referral Programs Increase Profits." *GfK Marketing Intelligence Review* 5, no. 1 (2013): 8–11. https://doi.org/10.2478/gfkmir-2014-0020

5 Schmitt, *et. al.*

- 92 percent of consumers around the world say they trust earned media, such as recommendations from friends and family, above all other forms of advertising.[6]
- Word of mouth is the primary factor behind 20 to 50 percent of all purchasing decisions.[7]

Earning Referrals

The KPIs on referrals break down in a very simple way:

- Conversion rate
- New customers
- CLV

Yes, your referral program impacts the CLV of referred customers, as well as the customers who refer them.

Here's a quote from my LinkedIn friend, Ben Cogan, on this:

"Marketers have a tendency to forget to include all relevant costs or overinflate CLV. But don't do the opposite!

The primary value of a customer is the profit she generates herself from her paid orders. Nothing new here.

But the other way a customer generates value is by referring her friends and family to your business. You should think of the profit that her referred friends generate as part of the CLV of the paid customer.

6 "Newswire: Consumer Trust in Online, Social and Mobile Advertising Grows." Nielsen, July 21, 2022. https://www.nielsen.com/insights/2012/consumer-trust-in-online-social-and-mobile-advertising-grows.

7 Bughin, Jacques, Jonathan Doogan, and Ole Jørgen Vetvik. "A New Way to Measure Word-of-Mouth Marketing." McKinsey & Company. McKinsey & Company, March 31, 2021. https://www.mckinsey.com/capabilities/growth-marketing-and-sales/our-insights/a-new-way-to-measure-word-of-mouth-marketing

At Hubble, we'd closely track the average number of customers that a paid customer referred (plus the average CLV of those customers). Across businesses, I've seen this referral rate range from 0.1x to 0.5x–meaning the average paid customer referred 0.1 to 0.5 other customers."

That's a lot, especially on the high end! But this isn't an academic point. The expected profit of the referred unpaid customers should count when making decisions on how much to pay to acquire a paid customer.

For example, if your average paid customer is referring to 0.25x other customers, and those customers have the same expected profit as the first customer, you should think of the CLV of the paid customer as 1.25x their direct profit.

Incidentally, it doesn't stop there–if the referred customers also themselves refer other customers, you should tack on the value of these 3rd-order customers too. Ad infinitum." Ben Cogan is the co-founder of Hubble Contacts, a DTC company that disrupts the eyewear industry by selling private label daily contact lenses sold directly to consumers through a subscription-based e-commerce business model. The company raised >$70M to date thanks to their data-driven approach.

One of the most important details to staging a successful referral program is timing. Unless your product is at the top of someone's mind, it's a long shot to ask them to refer your product or service to someone else.

Imagine you just bought a certain brand of cosmetics. The lipstick and nail polish haven't even arrived yet. How would you feel if this brand reached out to you through an automated email and invited you to refer them to someone else?

Strangely, a lot of companies operate this way. In my view, it's a sign of desperation, trying to pile acquisition on top of acquisition before a person has a feeling for you. As soon as a first-time purchase goes through, the customer's email lights up with a new referral-based offer. These shoppers can't advocate for something they haven't used. It's the exact opposite of a CLV-minded strategy. You're almost daring them to churn.

The fault does not fall completely on the companies that do this. Internet data shows plenty of cases where people openly talk about products they haven't used. One area involves online book reviews, where readers will even admit to not having finished a book as part of their review. Granted, online book reviews come with a certain amount of exposure, and some people want to get a boost in their social media status.

Referring a product to a friend or family member is different and usually happens privately. As a company, do you really want someone who hasn't used your product to be a voice for you?

A strategic referral program involves waiting until a customer becomes a habitual consumer. This person ranks high in your RFM segmentation. They love everything you offer and are constantly buying the same lotion, face cream, perfume, nail polish, you name it. They are way past the onboarding phase. These are your ultimate candidates to pull into a referral program.

Activating Your Referral Program

To activate your referral component, you need to have Soulmate and Lovers lined up and ready to go. How do you know if they are happy to refer your product to a friend? Easy! Let the NPS do some work for you.

- Ask Soulmates and Lovers how likely they are to recommend your products or services. You can do this in a targeted email or a quick survey at the bottom of a receipt from their next purchase.
- Once they share their high score, you can lead them into the referral program and provide the right incentive to share a referral.
- You can even provide a snippet of prefilled text they can share with their referral.

Make it Easy for People to Refer You

To capitalize on your referral program, create as frictionless an experience as possible. Remember, they are in love with your product and probably with your company. Do not complicate their lives or give them a lot of work to do. Let them join your referral program without feeling any pressure or having to deal with any complications.

What's in it for Them

There are all sorts of ways to generate word-of-mouth referrals. Whatever you do, you want to structure your referral program in a way that clearly shows customers what they get if they bring more business your way.

Some people who truly love you will jump at the chance to refer your products to friends of theirs. Others will need an incentive in order to promote you. You can offer them anything that's realistic for your business, including things like:

- Free products
- Credits for their future purchases (which also helps with retention)
- Discount codes they can share with other people
- Co-branded gifts from other companies that you partner with
- Gift cards related to your business, products, or even the product's JTBD

What you offer will be a matter of testing and improving things as you go on. As with so many other details related to CLV and customer-minded campaigns, your referral program is not a set-and-forget situation. Use certain incentives long enough, so you have enough data to measure their effectiveness. Review the implication, and decide how to amplify things going forward.

Launching Your Referral Program

The following visual outlines the steps to launching your referral program:

Referral programs are not for every business. In my experience, they tend to work best for aspirational-type products (apparel, cosmetics, fitness, etc.) or things people seek to accumulate or compound (certain tools, collectibles, cloud space, etc.) In either case, products or services that people have tried and tested and of which they have directly experienced the benefits work best for referrals.

I also want to point out a distinction between growth referral programs (within the traditional business), and the types of referrals that happen in multi-level-marketing (MLM) companies. For MLMs, referrals are their engine of growth. They create products, then focus on building their networks. From there, they leverage their networks in specific ways, and the goal is to build the network.

The types of referral programs I'm focusing on here are offshoots or part of after-growth strategies that happen in traditional business models. Here, it's not about the network of people but about the product.

Remember, RFM can be a big help when designing your referral program. For instance, if a customer has placed six orders, which puts them in the "high chance" category of placing yet another order, they make a better candidate for a referral program. Still, you will have to decide on what metrics make the most sense for you as you build your program. (More on this in the case study that follows.)

Whatever you decide, conduct the right type of customer hygiene first. The more you sort your categories, the better your chances are for success.

A Referral Program Case Study

In my previous life, I co-founded what became the largest online car insurance player in Romania. We had roughly a quarter million annual customers. At a certain time, we struggled to create new ideas to achieve profitability, despite our large volumes. That was when we calculated our paid media cost-per-order (a whopping $12) and decided to launch some new ideas based on this amount.

What did we do? We bought three thousand anniversary cakes and sent them to existing customers. Yes, we threaded the line between "insanity" and "genius." Lucky for us, it worked. Of course, a few variables helped us along:

- Winter was the high season for us. In December, most cars needed to renew their MTPL car insurance.
- We knew the anniversaries of these customers because we were meticulous in our data.
- We found a good Turkish baker who could handle such a big order.

We monitored the NPS and CAC and surveyed customers after purchase to understand how they'd heard about us. Before our great cake giveaway, about 12 percent of customers stated they heard about us from a friend or colleague. After the cakes, the figure shot up to 36 percent. Meanwhile, NPS increased by 17.5, and the overall CAC was 28 percent lower.

Other Referral Case Studies

Since we're all consumers on one level or another, we've probably referred a friend to a company or two over time.

In this spirit, I'd like to share a few short case studies from successful referral programs out in the world. You might be familiar with some of them.

Warby Parker

The eyewear company's referral program offered customers a $50 credit for each referred friend who made a purchase. This program led to a 50 percent increase in customer acquisition and a 20 percent increase in average order value for referred customers. David Gilboa, Warby Parker's co-founder, and co-CEO, stated in interviews that the referral program helped the company rapidly grow its customer base and increase the lifetime value of its customers. Today, their current strategy is to continue to provide undeniable value and increase their CLV. Not a bad plan.

Rent the Runway

The clothing rental service offered customers a $30 credit for each referred friend who signed up for the service. This program led to a 40 percent increase in customer acquisition and a 30 percent increase in customer lifetime value for referred customers.

Harry's

The men's grooming company offered customers a $5 credit for each referred friend who made a purchase. This program led to a 20 percent increase in customer acquisition and a 25 percent increase in customer lifetime value for referred customers.

Dropbox

In a fifteen-month span between 2008 and 2009, Dropbox grew from one hundred thousand registered users to four million. That's the growth of nearly 4,000 percent! Today, they are up to seven-hundred million users. Their referral program was the kickstart. Every three months, they doubled their user base. In April 2010, alone, their users sent nearly three million invites. The set-up for this program could not have been better. They were in the business of offering cloud storage space, and the program rewarded people with more free space in two ways: when they referred someone and when they accepted an invitation. This is known as a two-side referral program, where you win no matter what side of the referral you are on.

Having discussed and explored the possibilities that exist with referral initiatives, let's take a look at their close cousins — loyalty programs.

CHAPTER 13

The Highs and Lows of Loyalty Programs

Lots of companies see loyalty programs as being "magic bullets" to boost CLV. My opinion is a little different. Most loyalty programs don't pay attention to customer behavior, and when a program is misguided, it can be the same as shooting in the dark.

However, there are also companies that win the game thanks to their loyalty programs. As Neil Hoyne states in his incredibly well-written book, Converted, "If you look at the average lifetime value of an Amazon Prime customer, it's almost thirty times greater than that of an average retailer's customer."

With that said, let's take a look at some of the benefits a well-orchestrated loyalty program can create.

Obvious (And Not so Obvious) Benefits

Loyal and Engaged Customers

A well-designed loyalty program can help your loyal customers feel like you really care about them. That will encourage them to return for future purchases and reduce their chances of churning.

CLV Goes Up

A loyalty program is a way to offer customers rewards and incentives to keep coming back. When successful, it increases Customer Lifetime Value and drives more revenue over time (as long as you do the math properly...more on this shortly).

Gain More Known Customers

Often neglected, this might be the most under-valued benefit of a loyalty program. Having customers, you can identify, access, and connect with is a great achievement, especially during these challenging GDPR and high CAC times that omnichannel companies are going through.

Better Customer Data

Loyalty programs help you collect data on customer behavior, which gives you new insight into their preferences, needs, and spending habits. You can use this information to support future marketing strategies and product development.

Your company Can Stand Out

A successful loyalty program helps you differentiate from your competitors, attract new customers, and (of course) retain existing ones.

A Great Tool for Word-of-Mouth Marketing

Your loyalty program can be a gateway into some very power of word-of-mouth marketing and referrals. When customers feel that you are taking great care of them, they are more likely to tell other people about you. When new customers seek you out, rather than you having to find them, it significantly decreases your CACs.

Design Your Loyalty Program with Data

When you build your loyalty program around data, you support and validate or push back on and redirect your assumptions. If you are not able to start with data, then I advise you to skip the idea of a loyalty program until you are. This leads me to a couple of pitfalls that come with loyalty programs.

1. Customers Have to Care

First, there's a good chance that new customers will not care about your loyalty program. This is similar to something I shared in chapter 12 about referral programs. When customers are new to your brand or products, it may take time before they want to engage at deeper levels. For this reason, loyalty programs work best when you focus on these four RFM segments:

- Soulmates
- Lovers
- New Passions
- Not to Lose

	SOULMATES & LOVERS YOUR BEST CUSTOMERS - LOYAL & ACTIVE	NEW PASSIONS NEW CUSTOMERS WITH HIGH POTENTIAL	NOT TO LOSE GOOD CUSTOMERS THAT ARE AT RISK
	R: Highest F: Highest M: Highest	R: Highest F: Lowest M: Highest	R: High>medium F: Any M: High
LOYALTY INITIATIVES	✓	✓	✓

2. These Customers Already Love You

The second part of the pitfall comes down to the fact that these customers might already be hooked on your products or services. Do Soulmates need extra incentives to shop with you? The point being, your loyalty program may be relying on incentives that you don't need to use. You're basically giving a discount to people who happily pay full price.

Obviously, neither pitfall accounts for everyone or every situation, but they do cover a wide range. This brings me back to the importance of completing RFM segmentation and building a math-based model that helps you clarify costs, goals, and the potential for additional revenue a loyalty program might create.

Let the Market Drive Your Loyalty Program

When you construct your loyalty program around data, you are effectively letting the market tell you what choices to make. How do you do this? Below I've included a number of considerations to guide you as you dive into the math of the market:

- First, decide how much you can afford to put into the program and to potentially lose on account of the program. The core question here is: What is the financial impact of giving incentives to X group, and so on?
- For example, if you are making $20 per soulmate, is it worth giving these same customers a two-dollar incentive?
- From there, you must decide how many customers from the next rung down ("lovers") do you need to turn into soulmates in order to make your loyalty program viable.

For the sake of conversation, let's say that in the midst of these calculations, you discover that you have two thousand soulmate customers ("group A"), and five thousand lovers ("group B"). Here are your next steps:

- Send a survey to 500 people from group A to gather their insights regarding a potential loyalty program.
- From their answers, extract any patterns that show up in the feedback they share.

- If you don't see themes or patterns initially, go deeper. Look at each question as an individual idea, and extract any themes that begin to arise or expand the research to more customers
- Begin to build your loyalty program around these themes.

As you go forward, craft different packages and offers, and continue to do the work involved in validating your decisions. You might be surprised to discover that your loyalty program is actually creating new Soulmates by encouraging new purchasing patterns among customers in your Lovers group.

Here's an indicative proposal of how a loyalty program could look, by connecting different tiers with the RFM segments.

RFM Segment	*Loyalty tier*	*# of customers*	*% of Revenue*	*Customer Benefits*						
				Personal Assistant	**Free Delivery**	**Free Returns**	**Priority Support**	**Delivery Priority**	**Post-order courtesy call/text message**	**Maximum Affordable Discount**
Soulmates	Platinum	4322	17%	✔	✔	Forever	✔	✔	✔	17%
Lovers	Gold	6574	14%	✔	✔	6 months	✔	✔	✔	12%
Potential lovers	Silver	12456	9%			2 months	✔		✔	7%
About to dump you	Bronze	35908	10%			1 month	✔			5%
New Passions	Bronze	3455	10%			2 months	✔			11%
Apprentice	n/a	9870	9%							4%
Ex-Lovers, Don Juans & Breakups	n/a	88903	31%							12%

An interesting perspective is to analyze an already implemented loyalty program through the lens of RFM segments. You will usually find some surprises, most likely related to something like "Platinum" or "Gold" customers going away (those Ex-Lovers). This often happens when a company doesn't do a good job of letting customers know about any expiration dates attached to their loyalty program (more on this below).

Avoid These Traps

Earlier, I mentioned pitfalls. Now I'd like to share some traps to avoid when you run a loyalty program.

Don't Set It and Forget It

When you launch a loyalty program, you might have some KPIs in mind. However, most companies don't monitor the impact properly. To validate that your loyalty program is working, you have to constantly monitor the following:

- CLV by RFM segment, and CLV by membership level. Are they going up?
- RFM segment transitions. Are more of your existing customers moving into the Soulmates and Lovers categories?
- More identifiable customers. What percentage of transactions are coming from known customers? (Hint: the more, the better.)

Forget About Vanity Metrics

It doesn't matter how many customers have your loyalty card, or have enrolled in your program. Are they actually using it? Are they still happy about it? Is your company thriving on account of it? Again, you must constantly monitor and optimize adoption and usage rate. These numbers matter more than just how many people have signed up.

Don't Be Afraid to Change

Just because you've launched a loyalty program doesn't mean you can't alter things when you need to. If customers don't use their rewards or spend loyalty points, don't advocate for your company, and aren't buying more than they used to, change things. A good loyalty program is an ongoing experiment!

Set and Share Expiration Dates

The power of scarcity is a real thing. If you're offering loyalty points or store credits, make sure they come with expiration dates, and that your customers know about them. A timely prompt can make a difference.

Know the Difference Between Perceived and Actual Value

When online retailers consider loyalty benefits, the idea of free delivery usually comes up. Sounds boring, right? Actually, this is an example of a great benefit. It includes a direct, economic value to your customers that is much higher than, say, the value of offering a "free return" policy, especially if you have a low return rate.

Use Your Program as a Way to Ask

Loyalty programs are about rewarding customers. However, some companies use loyalty programs as a way to ask your most loyal customers to pay upfront for future purchases. In these types of paid loyalty programs, your customers are essentially paying you to make it even easier for them to purchase their products on a regularly scheduled basis.

Amazon Prime is a good example. Did you know that the average CLV for Prime members is nearly $2,300? That's more than twice the CLV for non-Prime subscribers.[8] Shoppers are

---

8 Bughin, Jacques, Jonathan Doogan, and Ole Jørgen Vetvik. "A New Way to Measure Word-of-Mouth Marketing." McKinsey & Company. March 31, 2021. https://www.mckinsey.com/capabilities/growth-marketing-and-sales/our-insights/a-new-way-to-measure-word-of-mouth-marketing

increasingly willing to pay for better benefits, with 37 percent of consumers affirming they would pay a fee for enhanced program benefits.

A Loyalty Program Case Study

As with the referral program case studies from chapter 11, I'd like to share another case study that you may be familiar with. This one involves Restoration Hardware (RH as they're known.) The company sells high-end home furnishings online, in galleries, and in outlet stores throughout North America. They also operate restaurants inside a select number of stores in the U.S.

In 2016, they launched their RH Grey Card loyalty program, effectively doing away with discount sales in the process. You can read a short review of their program on RetailDive.com.[9] For an annual fee of $100, customers take advantage of a 25 percent discount off items in any department, 10 percent off discount items, and other perks as well. If someone plans to spend $400 or more a year, then the program pays for itself.

Charging a fee was a major decision for them but not unprecedented. Consider companies like Amazon or Costco, which also charge an annual fee for memberships. With RH, one of the differences is that their customer base is more affluent, and their furnishings are higher-end. For these customers, spending a nominal fee to save a few hundred dollars makes sense. Not everyone can afford a hundred-dollar annual fee, but RH's metrics determined that this was the ideal price point for their customer base.

---

9 Howland, Daphne. "Restoration Hardware Launches Paid Membership Program, Ends Sales." Retail Dive, March 29, 2016. https://www.retaildive.com/news/restoration-hardware-launches-paid-membership-program-ends-sales/416423

Did it work? Yes, incredibly well. To date, 400,000 members have signed up for the program. Combined, these members drive 95 percent of sales. Plus, income from memberships actually grew faster than sales when they launched the program. Even better for RH, their stock price grew tenfold, going from around $30 to over $300 at the time of this writing.

Now that I have shared the potential ups and downs of a loyalty program, let's jump into our last phase of a customer's journey and discuss ways to bring old flames back.

CHAPTER 14

Bring Back Your Old Flames

Just because a customer's gone doesn't mean you have to forget them. Maybe you're one message away from bringing them back. That's what reactivation initiatives are all about.

Customers who fall into the reactivation category are the last percentile of those who could potentially come back to your business. That makes these initiatives less effective than the others I've discussed in part 3.

	EX-LOVERS FORMER BEST CUSTOMERS THAT ARE INACTIVE	DON JUANS FORMER HIGH POTENTIAL CUSTOMERS (NEW PASSIONS) THAT ARE INACTIVE	BREAKUPS FORMER AVERAGE CUSTOMERS THAT ARE INACTIVE
	R: Lowest F: Highest M: Highest	R: Lowest F: Lowest M: Highest	R: Lowest F: Low - Average M: Low -Average
REACTIVATION INITIATIVES	✓	✓	✓

Even though reactivations aren't where most companies spend too much time or capital, a reactivation initiative can bring considerable benefits if done right. But just to be clear, the best way to run a reactivation initiative is to avoid doing it at all. Don't let your customers land in this category. Okay, let's ignore this pipe dream for a minute and get down to the most critical details of making reactivations work.

Timing is Key

Let's assume that some of your former Soulmates are going to run out on you for some reason. Despite the time, effort, and resources you put into improving your acquisition efforts, nurturing the onboarding process, and maintaining good connections, they're gone. If you've stayed with the CVO methodology to this point, then you can continue to use data and customer insights to guide your reactivation process. When you do, keep an eye on timing.

It's always nice to say hello to customers, even if they've been gone for a bit. Maybe that's all it takes to flip the switch and bring them back. It might have nothing to do with the product or even their experience. People get busy and sometimes forget.

Is there a "right" time to do this? Here's an example of a company where most Soulmates follow a 30-day buying window between purchases. The purchasing window is unique to every business, but I'll use this timing for the sake of conversation.

- If the 30-day window comes and goes, customer X falls into the prevention category.

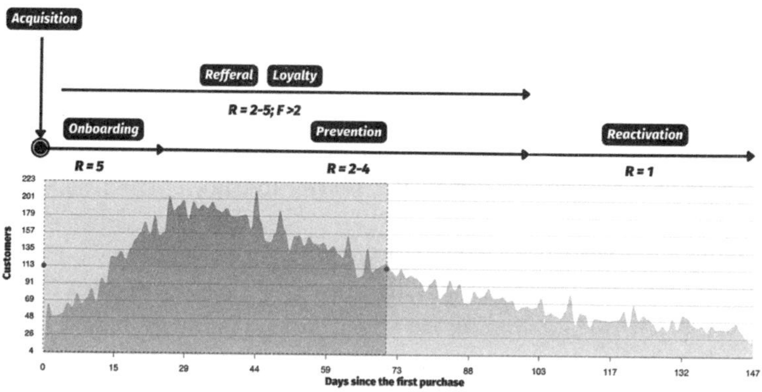

- Perhaps you allow a customer to linger in prevention territory for another 30 days. It's up to you to decide how long before they move from prevention to reactivation. This depends on how you define Recency scores when you set up RFM segmentation.
- Usually, reactivation is for customers that are in the last percentile of Recency scores. Maybe you need to reconsider your windows of time before someone slips into reactivation land. Don't worry, you can always adjust RFM scores.

- You also want to determine whether to include a lull period, which links up with the prevention strategy I covered in chapter 11. Some companies will pause prevention, then let a period of silence go by before they start reactivation. This can depend on the products you sell. For slow-moving consumer goods, you probably don't need to be too pushy with messaging. For faster-moving products, you want to stay top-of-mind with relevant, appealing messages.

The Importance of Knowing Why

In many ways, reactivation lives on the opposite side of the acquisition coin. However, you can't necessarily think of reactivation as a "re-acquisition" initiative. In acquisition, you focus on three components: target (channel & customer), offer (the product, price, promotion), and message (the creative). Should you follow this same pattern for reactivation? No. In fact, if you do, you'll probably miss the mark.

True, you need all three components to make reactivation work, but you can't just try to blast old customers back into loving you. Take a look at these survey results below, for example, from a real company:

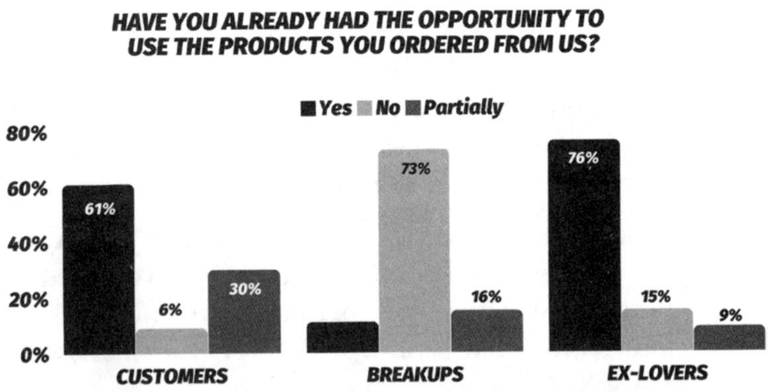

What you notice when you look at the survey results is that most low-value customers haven't actually used the product this company sells (low-carb keto snack). Why did they buy it in the first place? Why did they stop buying? I'll come back to this chart and the company during the chapter's case study.

Unlocking the mystery of "Why?" is the most important detail. Since you're smart and you've read 95 percent of this book, you've done your customer research the right way.

You'll already know the reasons behind every "Why?" when it's time to reactivate your customers. You'll have an unfair position against all of your competitors, who will continue to blindly throw things at the wall. They'll promise better prices, new ways to save, or some other shiny detail. Too bad for them that their old customers won't care.

When reactivation initiatives follow the spray and pray model, it's a sign that a company isn't thinking strategically. They're just doing something because they think they should. No matter what campaign initiative you're looking at, strategy is king, even when the stakes are low, as they are with reactivation. Your message must follow suit. Just because sales are dropping and Soulmates have disappeared doesn't mean you should flood everyone's inboxes with discounts. This will only harm the perception of your brand.

Based on all of the CVO methodology you have followed to date, you should already know the job that your soulmate customers want your product to perform. Is the fact that Soulmates have gone away a sign that the product has stopped working? Was there a moment when things began to drop off? What can you discern if you go back and reexamine the insights from the NPS responses?

The Trojan Horse Reactivation Method

When you get a discount code out of the blue from a company you've forgotten about, what's your move? Do you jump at the chance to spend money? Do you scratch your head and wonder why you're still on the email list? For me, when this happens, I usually ignore it. At best, I'll scan the offer and wonder if I did something to deserve it.

This brings to mind a technique I like to call the Trojan Horse method. I have used this for my own businesses and for clients many times, and it works more often than not. In a nutshell, here's a visual that shows how it goes:

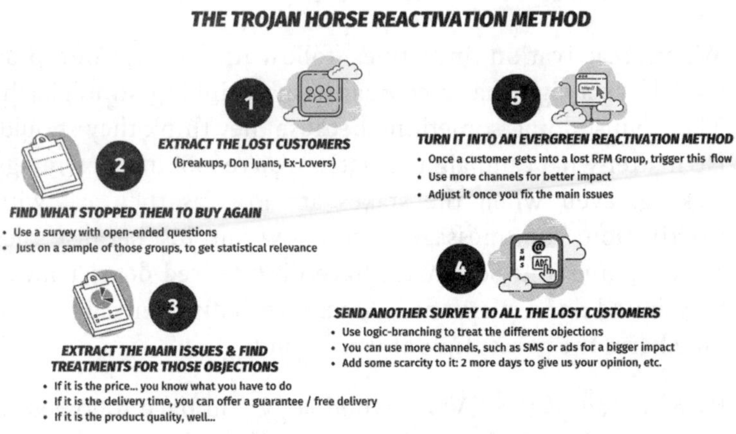

What do you think? Mind blown? Kind of? A little? One important detail is the fact that this method will also feed you with ongoing insights about the drop reasons. That's why you have to add the "other reason" as an open-ended answer in any survey you send out. It's a window into new issues that might cause customers to ditch you.

A Reactivation Case Study

Believe it or not, the key to reactivation (which is to avoid it in the first place) begins during customer onboarding. All of the case studies I've shared throughout part 3 end on happy notes. Time to be a downer! It's the story of the low-carb/keto company I teased a few pages ago with the chart that shows Customers, Breakups, and Ex-Lovers. Why were so many New Passions winding up in the reactivation bin?

A reactivation initiative begins when you're sure a customer is gone but before they unsubscribe from your email list. Once again, it all comes down to timing, and you hold those keys. If you allow too much time to pass since their last purchase, a reactivation campaign can actually feel like a last-ditch effort. You don't want this. You want to keep customers close and connected.

I like to get my hands dirty when I'm working with companies to understand how to bring undeniable value to them via our technology and training opportunities. As the saying goes, you have to eat the food to know how it really tastes.

My firm and I jumped into the most thorough level of research we could for our keto client. Their main concern was that more than 120,000 previous customers hadn't bought from them in a year. They wanted ALL OF THEM back. Kind of a big lift, but we were up for the challenge.

We started with RFM analysis, continued with surveys, and quickly realized a few interesting things (not to mention how odd it was that so many Breakups never used their product, to begin with). Take a look at the chart below:

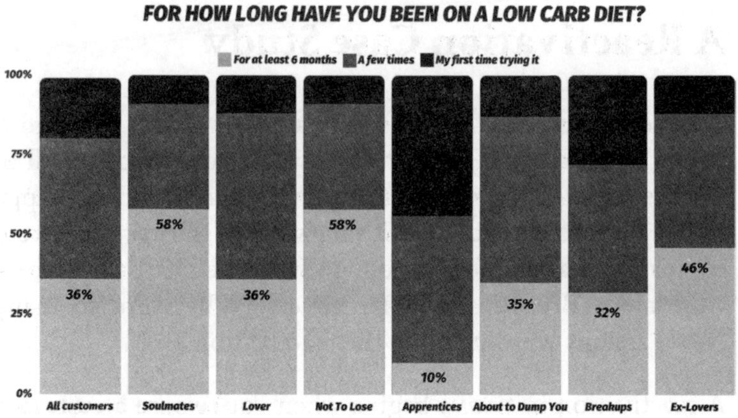

As you can see, the majority of Soulmates and Not To Lose customers had been eating a low-carb diet for at least six months, while almost half of the Ex-Lovers were as well. This led to a question: if the product is good, why are so many Ex-Lovers jumping ship? We zeroed in on two variables, price, and taste. Here's what we asked and what we found:

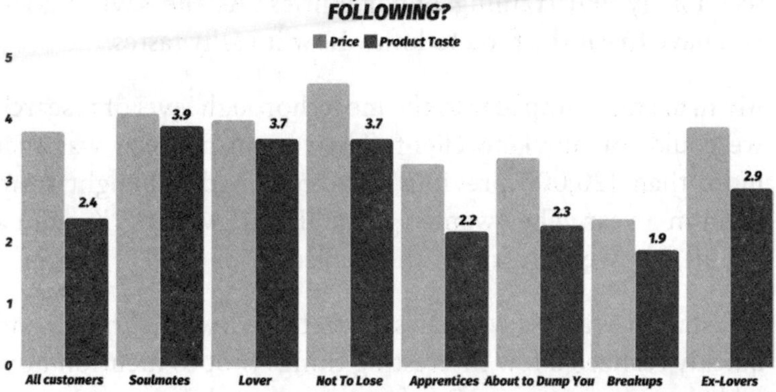

Across the board, most customers felt pretty good about the price, with Breakups clocking in the lowest score. As for taste, Soulmates ranked it the highest, followed by Lovers and Not to Lose. But look at those pesky Ex-Lovers! This was our lightbulb moment. Something was off about how the product tasted, even for a segment of customers (Ex-Lovers) where almost half had been eating a low-carb diet for at least six months.

Pop quiz: Can marketing fix a broken product? (You know the answer.)

Get Started with Reactivation

Be warned that most reactivation initiatives are less than 10 percent effective. But since they are low effort, even with a mid-low impact, they are still worth it for plenty of businesses. Are you one of those businesses? If you have a large number of "gone" customers, and the research tells you that the problem is fixable, then the answer is yes.

I don't mean to cry in my low-carb keto snack, but reactivation campaigns have the largest customer target. It's a sad fact of life, my friend, especially if you have been churning and burning. So please keep the following in mind before you launch into reactivation mode:

- Your RFM segmentation will show you the way forward. Trust your work.
- Do you want every one-time customer back, or do you only want to engage with old Soulmates and Ex-Lovers? Not all customers leave for the same reasons.
- Recency is still the best indicator of a future purchase. Customers who purchased six months ago may be more interested in coming back than someone who hasn't purchased from you in a year or so.

You know where to go for the data, insights, and tools you need to run all of these distinctive CVO initiatives. Here's the link.

www.theCLVrevolution.com

Conclusion

Writing a book about a moving target has been an exciting, challenging (sometimes even painful) endeavor.

As you have discovered the power of focusing on providing undeniable value to your customers, I hope you'll practice, improve and share this method further.

My vision is that in a few years from now, retailers will genuinely care about their customers and will guide their decisions by customer lifetime value, which will be their North Star Metric. Their teams and service providers focus on their customers' actions and feelings, orchestrating relevant customer journeys.

On the other hand, I know there are very tiny chances that eCommerce experts and agencies will continue to survive while ignoring customer lifetime value optimization.

You've done a lot of work, and I'd like to take this moment to congratulate you. This book has asked you to be diligent, creative, and thoughtful; it's asked you to delve into your data, launch you into building a platform to conduct critical interviews, and provide you with tools and resources you can use immediately. Beyond all of that, it has also reminded you that all businesses, including yours, are about the people whose needs, problems, and challenges you solve. I genuinely hope and urge you to use the knowledge you got from this book to be a force of good and help people make actual progress. From an ethical perspective, I hope you'll use your conscience to use the knowledge and help companies that provide real value, helping their customers make real progress, not get stuck in addictive and harmful behaviors.

For that matter, the same is true for my business - we don't work with companies from industries like adult, tobacco, guns, or gambling.

So let me say two things:

1. Thank you for staying with this book and the work I have asked you to do.
2. I hope that this book has done the job that you needed it to perform.

Neither of these points is lip service, and I want you to know that I am always open to your feedback, thoughts, notes, and ideas for how we can continue to extend the work and the reach of CVO Academy, as well as the benefits of this book. If you need more, you can hear more from me if you search for my podcast CVO Live. reach me through the dedicated CLV Revolution web portal or on LinkedIn. As you're already part of the CVO movement, I'd love to be able to help you make progress, as that was the job to be done by my book.

As I wrap up this book, I want to remind you of something very critical that I shared at the start: CVO is not a "set-it-and-forget-it" proposition. You have to maintain quality over time. If you want to nail CVO again and again, you will continue to do the following:

- Avoid traps and confirmation biases. There's nothing wrong with "trusting your gut", as long as you have the data to support your feelings.
- Continue to troubleshoot with experts and build a team of professionals to manage various aspects of the CVO methodology. Going alone will not get you as far as going together.
- Revisit the ups and downs you experience. There is always meaning hiding in the numbers. Don't be afraid to sift through the bad times to find something important.

- As you do, tend to the stuck or squeaky wheels that happen along the way. Some might need grease, while others will need to be replaced.

Finally, remember that you must be willing to adapt and maintain a flexible mindset seeking to optimize. Being in business is not the same as being in the game of bribing your customers with discounts again and again as a way to drum up repeat business or relying exclusively on great creativity so you can offset churn through acquisition only. The change you want to achieve begins with changing your own mind and inspiring others in your organization to change theirs. You'll be surprised at what happens when you let customers lead the way.

Or, since you've engaged so heavily in the CVO methodology, maybe you won't be surprised. Maybe you already know the power that your customers hold.

I believe that you do. Here's to your success!

PS: Allow me to eat my own dog food: on a scale from 0 to 10, what are the chances of recommending this book to a friend or colleague?

BIT.LY/HOW-LIKELY-ARE-YOU

About the Author

Valentin is one of the principal architects of the Customer Value Optimization methodology, the Founder of Omniconvert, and the Founder of The CVO Academy.

Growing up as a poor kid in Bucharest, Romania, Valentin Radu learned early the importance of underpromising and over-delivering to succeed in life.

Always driven to create value, he lives by the principle that in order to get value, you must first give it to others. This helped him build 4 companies with various degrees of success and make a name for himself in the global eComm and entrepreneurial world.

Currently, he is the founder and CEO of Omniconvert and The CVO Academy. His company provides growth solutions to hundreds of retail companies that are willing to become customer-centric and train agencies willing to provide services to their customers. Some of these companies are Decathlon, Tempur, or Orange.

Today Radu is the mind behind the CVO movement: he launched the CVO Academy with prominent professors and practitioners that teach people how to achieve sustainable growth by understanding and caring about their customers.

Acknowledgments

We're living in this amazing world, but our eyes can't see all the causes that led to what we experience.

This book is the fruit of so many struggles, interactions, collaborations, learnings, mistakes, and life experiences that made it possible.

I used to identify as a poor kid coming from Berceni, Bucharest, Romania, an ex-communist country. I have received so much help from people all over the world that made it impossible for me to mention them all. I wrote this book with the clear intention of helping others and passing this knowledge in a coherent way. That was possible thanks to so many people, and I feel gratitude, respect,and deep appreciation for everyone that has influenced me, consciously or not, positive or not. THANK YOU!

That said, I have to thank a few very specific people that helped me write this book. I want to thank my dear soulmate Camelia: you always see the good in me, and I am growing and paying it forward thanks to you. I love you!

I want to thank my family. Having a loving family is my life's treasure. To my father, Stefan: your resilience made me overcome all the obstacles. You are my true hero. To my loving mother, Maria. Your love taught me to always know that there's always a bright place to go back to. To my amazing kids,

Stefan and Sarra, and my sisters, Gabriela and Aura. Thanks for supporting me when I had more energy than anyone could handle.

I want to thank Maria for being my business partner and integrator for almost a decade. We create meaningful change when we work together.

I want to thank the many mentors who have guided or inspired me, Florian Colceag, Doina Badiu, Gina Calagiu, Christian Goldmann, and Bob Moesta. I also want to thank the bright minds that I was inspired by: professor Peter Fader, professor Daniel McCarthy, Dennis Yu, Karl Gilis, Val Geisler, Chase Dimond, Kurt Elster, Drew Sanocki, Ben Cogan, Jesse Horwitz, and Tim Kilroy.

To my coworkers at Omniconvert and the people who I've worked with throughout the years, especially Teodor Rogojina, Sorin Enache, Matei Lungu, Georgiana Atanasiu, Vladi Iancu, Oana Predoiu, Oana Andruc, Tania Grigore, Laura Ruczui, Laurentiu Balasa, Marius Ghenea, Teo Serban, Alex Volocaru, Cristi Movila, Dragos Brinza, Octavian Stefan, Adelina Badea, Hermina Manole, Raluca Ene, Thomas Robson-Kanu, Alex Pintilie, Eugen Birgaoanu, Mara Gavrilescu, Horatiu Mitu, Anca Sandu, Vasile Darie, Radu Vrabie, Mihai Chitic, Sorin Dumitrescu, Cristian Lupu, Irina, and Juliana Jackson: thank you, all!

I want to thank my best students and agency partners that join me in the CVO movement: Adam Pearce, Peter Gardner, Julien Normand, Afif Ghannoum, Omar Lovert, Adam Kitchen, Ben Fitzpatrick, Ales Pokora, Alexandra Cho, Ward Carey, Jim Martin, and Robert Ribciuc.

I want to thank the people from Scribe Media who worked on this book: Sophie May, Lauren Smith, Miles Rote, JeVon McCormick and of course, Dave Jarecki, my scribe. Dave, you are a monument of patience and inspiration, and I am grateful for being able to work with you! This book is the result of so many experiences, and I am grateful to everyone who made it possible. Thank You!